Introduction to Real Estate Sales
For Fiduciaries

By
Orit Gadish

Copyright © 2023

Orit Gadish – All Rights Reserved

This book may not be reproduced without the written permission of the author and publisher.

Printed in the United States of America

ISBN 978-1-954713-24-6

BH4 Publishing

About the Author

Orit Gadish is the Broker/Owner of Geffen Real Estate, with a successful track record of selling over 1,450 properties, both commercial and residential, over the past 18 years, throughout the state of California. Orit oversees a team of 30 agents, providing them with guidance and support. Her in-depth experience in this space leads to the depth you will experience in this book.

Orit has also had a long and successful career in the corporate world, in the consulting space, helping businesses to streamline their operations by designing, developing, and implementing improved business processes and software solutions to increase their bottom line. She served in an executive role at Countrywide Financial, both as a Vice President to help launch and grow a new Joint Venture Division and later as First Vice President of their Internet Channel Management division. Orit's management and technical abilities are reflected in the highly structured processes outlined in this book.

Orit is a graduate of the University of California at Santa Barbara. She holds a degree in political science and another in computer science. Orit resides in Beverly Hills, on a fruit tree farm, with her husband and four daughters.

Motivation

As a real estate broker, I bear the fiduciary duty of utmost care, integrity, honesty, and loyalty in dealings with my clients, similar to the responsibilities that a doctor and a lawyer have to their patients and clients. When I transitioned to serve those in a fiduciary capacity, my duty of care drove me to look for answers, conduct research, and understand the processes and how real estate is handled and sold within this new space. I could not find information discussing how to effectively transact real estate within this space, so as I gained the experience myself, I would take notes, document my observations, actions taken by all parties, and develop my procedures. I finally decided to compile notes over time and organized them into this book to clarify the process for those looking for it.

This book is intended to serve as a resource for newer practitioners who serve in fiduciary capacity. Seasoned professionals in a fiduciary capacity can utilize this book as part of their training program when onboarding newer members into their team.

Practitioners in a fiduciary capacity, dispose of real estate with the help of real estate agents (see figure below). This book looks at the relationships and processes between these stakeholders with much detail as it relates to the sale of real estate.

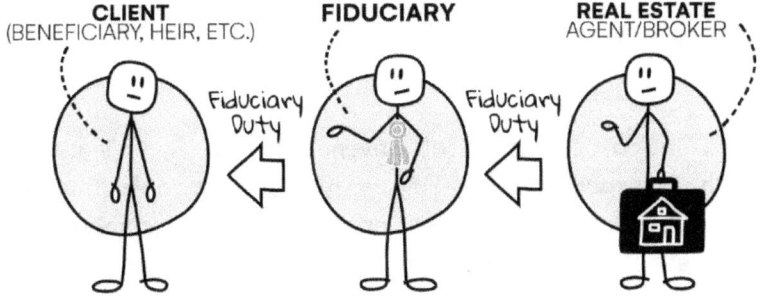

Note that I am not an attorney. The content of this book should not be considered legal advice. You should always consult with your attorney or CPA before making decisions and taking action. These are general guidelines for the state of California, and please note that there are variations within the various regions and courts of California. If you are operating outside of the state of California, please consult with an attorney and CPA who practices in that state for state-specific laws and procedures.

Overview

This book is comprised of eleven chapters. It reflects the author's experiences working with fiduciaries, on residential and commercial real estate sales, brokerage management, and business process management.

Chapter 1: Selecting Your Real Estate Agent

Chapter 2: Setting Expectations with Your Agent

Chapter 3: Pre-Marketing Strategies

Chapter 4: Cash for Keys Process and Agreement

Chapter 5: The Eviction Process

Chapter 6: Getting the Property Ready for Market

Chapter 7: Valuing the Property

Chapter 8: Marketing the Property

Chapter 9: Purchase Agreement Terms

Chapter 10: Offer Management

Chapter 11: Closing and Settlement

Legal Disclaimer

Although the author and publisher made every effort to ensure that this book's information was accurate at press time, the author and publisher do not assume and hereby disclaim any liability to any party for any loss, damage, or disruption caused by errors or omissions.

The author and the publisher disclaim all liability to the maximum extent permitted by law if any information, analysis, opinions, advice, or recommendations in this book prove inaccurate, incomplete, unreliable, or result in any other losses.

The information contained in this book does not constitute legal or financial advice and should never be used without first consulting with legal and other professionals.

The publisher and the author do not make any guarantee or other promise as to any outcomes that may or may not be obtained from using this book's content. You should conduct your research and due diligence.

The information provided throughout this book is on California-specific and may or may not apply in your state. Also, local courts within the state of California have varying procedures and forms to be used. Rules and regulations referenced in this book are subject to change.

Brief Table of Contents

About the Author 3

Motivation 4

Overview 6

Legal Disclaimer 7

Brief Table of Contents 8

Table of Contents 9

Chapter 1: Selecting Your Real Estate Agent 15

Chapter 2: Setting Expectations with Your Agent 20

Chapter 3: Pre-Marketing Strategies 29

Chapter 4: Cash for Keys Process and Agreement 41

Chapter 5: The Eviction Process 49

Chapter 6: Getting the Property Ready for Market 66

Chapter 7: Valuing the Property 78

Chapter 8: Marketing the Property 84

Chapter 9: Purchase Agreement Terms 97

Chapter 10: Offer Management 103

Chapter 11: Closing and Settlement 111

Table of Contents

About the Author 3
Motivation 4
Overview 6
Legal Disclaimer 7
Brief Table of Contents 8
Table of Contents 9
Chapter 1: Selecting Your Real Estate Agent 15
    Chapter Overview 15
    Chapter Outline 15
    Introduction 16
    Empathetic Mindset 16
    Desire to Learn 17
    Motivated and Proactive 17
    Relationship-Minded 18
    Grit and Resilience 18
    Dysfunctional Tendencies 18
Chapter 2: Setting Expectations with Your Agent 20
    Chapter Overview 20
    Chapter Outline 20
    Introduction 21
    Team Expectations 21
    Marketing Strategy Expectations 22
    Pricing Expectations 24

Scope Expectations 25

Reporting Expectations 26

Chapter 3: Pre-Marketing Strategies 29

Chapter Overview 29

Chapter Outline 29

Introduction 30

Understanding the Current Situation 30

Deciding on the Marketing Strategy 30

    Vacant Units...30

    Occupied Units..34

Chapter 4: Cash for Keys Process and Agreement 41

Chapter Overview 41

Chapter Outline 41

Introduction 42

The Cash for Keys Process..42

    Due Diligence: Location and Local Requirements (Step 1) 43

    Determining Initial CFK Terms (Step 2)..............................43

    Making Contact with Occupant (Step 3) 43

    Negotiating Relocation/CFK Terms (Step 4) 44

    Executing the Cash for Keys Agreement (Step 5)..............45

    Property Inspection and Delivery of Payment (Step 6)......45

The Cash for Keys Agreement...46

Chapter 5: The Eviction Process 49

Chapter Overview 49

Chapter Outline 49

Introduction 51

Summary of the Eviction Process 52

Issuing Notice to Terminate Tenancy (Step 1) 53

    Giving Notice for At Fault 53

    Giving Notice for No-Fault 55

Filing an Unlawful Detainer Summons and Complaint (Step 2) 57

Tenant Responds to Complaint? (Decision Point D1) 58

Court Hearing (Step 3a) 58

Set for Trial, Settlement Conference, and Trial (Step 3b) 58

Landlord Favored? (Decision Point D2) 59

Tenant Files Demand for Jury Trial (Decision Point D3) 59

Landlord Files for Default Judgement (Step 3) 59

Writ of Possession Issued (Step 4) 59

Sheriff Posts Notice (Step 5) 60

Sheriff Lockout (Step 6) 60

Documenting Personal Property Left Behind (Step 7) 60

Delivering Notice of Right to Reclaim Abandoned Personal Property (Step 8) 60

Storing Abandoned Property (Step 9) 63

Personal Property Claimed? (Decision Point D4) 63

Releasing Abandoned Property (Step 10) 63

Conducting a Public Sale of Personal Property (Step 11) 64

Handling Sale Proceeds 64

Handling Abandoned Vehicles 64

Handling Squatters 65

Chapter 6: Getting the Property Ready for Market 66

Chapter Overview 66

Chapter Outline 66

Introduction 68

Assigning Responsibilities 68

Rekeying and Securing the Property 68

Initial Property Inspection 69

Personal Property Disposition 70

Utilities 70

Initial and Ongoing Maintenance 71

    Initial and Ongoing Sales Clean 71

    Initial and Ongoing Yard Maintenance 72

    Initial and Ongoing Pool Maintenance 73

    Initial and Ongoing Handling of Safety and Habitability Issues 73

    Initial Winterization 74

    Ongoing Snow Removal 75

    Initial Removal of Distractions 75

    Ongoing Handling of Emergencies 76

Renovations 77

Chapter 7: Valuing the Property 78

Chapter Overview 78

Chapter Outline 78

Introduction 79

Broker Price Opinion (BPO) AKA Comparative Market Analysis (CMA) 79

Broker Opinion of Value (BOV) 81

Determining a List Price 82
Chapter 8: Marketing the Property 84
    Chapter Overview 84
    Chapter Outline 84
    Introduction 85
    Signage 86
    Professional Photos of Property 87
    Property Description 88
    Professional Video and 3D Virtual Tour 89
    Professional Website 90
    Placing Property on MLS, LoopNet, CoStar 90
    Listing Printout 91
        Public Remarks 91
        Private Remarks 92
        Showing Properties 92
    Conducting Open Houses 93
    Traditional Marketing 94
    Online Marketing 95
    Handling Price Reductions 95
Chapter 9: Purchase Agreement Terms 97
    Chapter Overview 97
    Chapter Outline 97
    Introduction 97
        As-Is Sales 98
        Investigations 100
        Warranties, Guarantees, or Representations 100

Requests for Repairs 100

Retrofitting Repairs 100

Escrow, Title, and Natural Hazard Disclosures (NHD) Vendors 101

Earnest Money Deposit 101

Buyer Inspections and Investigations 102

Extension of Time Addendum and Per Diem Fee 102

Chapter 10: Offer Management 103

Chapter Overview 103

Chapter Outline 104

Introduction 105

Offer Submission Instructions 105

Reviewing and Processing Offers 106

Handling Multiple Offer Situations 107

The Contract Package 109

Contract Package Review 109

Chapter 11: Closing and Settlement 111

Chapter Overview 111

Chapter Outline 111

Introduction 113

The Escrow Process 113

Pre-Escrow Period Activities (Phase 1): 114

Initial Escrow Period Activities (Phase 2): 121

Intermediate Escrow Period Activities (Phase 3) 122

End of Escrow Period Activities (Phase 4): 126

Pending to Sold Activities (Phase 5) 130

Chapter 1: Selecting Your Real Estate Agent

Chapter Overview

How do you identify the right real estate agent to hire to help you with selling the real estate you are handling in a fiduciary capacity? What types of skills and abilities are essential? This chapter discusses various attributes that your agent should possess to contribute to a successful sale.

Chapter Outline

Empathetic Mindset

Desire to Learn

Motivated and Proactive

Relationship-Minded

Grit and Resilience

Dysfunctional Tendencies

Introduction

You have one or more real estate assets that that needs to be sold, and you need to assign it to a real estate agent to sell them for you. Your ideal agent will be empathetic and patient and possess intelligence and good judgment, which develops from relevant experience and knowledge of the real estate, working with fiduciaries and exemplary personal qualities that allow the agent to make the right decisions.

You want to surround yourself with the best possible talent available to you. It has been proven that if you surround yourself with driven leaders, you become a better leader yourself. Hiring the best people will allow you to have sufficient time to focus on your responsibilities and duties to your client and to deliver excellent results.

Empathetic Mindset

The empathetic agent will take the time to understand what exactly is happening in your situation. Your agent should be able to think about the pains that each person involved in the case may be suffering and to feel for them. Your agent will be able to understand another human being, mind to mind, and be able to think about other people first before making decisions. Your agent should know how to communicate with them in a way that calms their anxiety, fears, and dissonance. An agent with an empathetic mindset knows when to offer condolences or encouragement and should know how to approach conversations in a mindful way that promotes cooperation.

Desire to Learn

Those with a desire to learn have a growth mindset, proactively seek learning from every situation, and have a desire to improve continuously. They can positively engage amid challenges and are open to feedback. They are self-aware and have better business judgment. An agent with these personal qualities is one that you can rely on and with whom you can develop a long-term relationship.

Motivated and Proactive

An agent who is motivated can accomplish the work that needs to get done and creates trust and commitment. There is a drive to get things done, along with high energy and a balanced ego. A balanced ego comes with confidence, being self-assured of one's abilities, humility, being modest, or having a low view of one's importance. Your agent should be people-centric, care about you and your client, and create a high commitment culture within your team. Also, the agent will have a strong vendor relationship with a network of vendors that can deliver effective solutions to remediate any issue with a property.

A proactive agent will desire to seek out potential overbidders, do the proper follow up with potential buyers, and invite them to the court hearing to overbid. Taking these extra steps will ensure that your agent is protecting your client's best interests and obtaining the highest possible return on the property's sale.

Relationship-Minded

A relationship-minded agent is concerned with long-term relationships, not transactional relationships where the immediate reward such as the commission is the only factor in the decision. This type of agent has the perspective that there are multiple stakeholders involved in each transaction. The agent desires to understand each stakeholder's values and purpose and then adopt strategies and practices that adhere to them.

Grit and Resilience

Grit and resilience will drive your agent to be proactive and take on responsibility preemptively to progress without direction from others. The agent will stay abreast of local, state, and federal laws. This agent will hold themselves and others accountable for completing assignments and achieving goals while overcoming any setbacks or failures that occur along the way. The agent will respond quickly, communicate effectively, and apply best practices. This agent will be enthusiastic and optimistic. This agent would require a certain grit that results in the agent's constant accomplishment and ongoing success in executing the proper strategy and plan.

Dysfunctional Tendencies

Those with dysfunctional tendencies such as being risk-averse, avoidant, and argumentative fear failure and become insecure. They do not possess the personality traits that will serve your client's best interest and will not be easy to work with.

Chapter 2: Setting Expectations with Your Agent

Chapter Overview

You have selected your real estate agent to join you on your journey to successfully sell the real property that is part of the estate and ensure that your clients are pleased with the outcome. Open communication is critical to make this happen, as you meet with your agent to define the scope of their responsibilities and set the proper expectations on a multitude of related topics.

Chapter Outline

Introduction

Team Expectations

Marketing Strategy Expectations

Pricing Expectations

Scope Expectations

Reporting Expectations

Introduction

Given the ideal personality traits and skills that your agent possesses, which were previously described, your agent would have the ability to develop and cultivate relationships with vendors and buyer's agents and work with you and your team in partnership to ensure all of your needs are met.

Throughout the real estate sales process, your agent should make recommendations for the best course of action to optimize the net sales proceeds and reduce the days on the market. This requires your agent to be proactive.

Your selected agent should be transparent about the real estate process and keep you updated throughout. Your agent's goals should be to make your life easier, and your agent should be easy to work with. It is essential that you schedule a meeting with your agent at the time of property assignment to discuss and review the items below. It is crucial to discuss your needs with your agent and set your expectations, which will ensure a successful real estate transaction.

Team Expectations

Communicating your team's expectations to your agent is critical in the successful sale of real estate. Introduce your agent to the team members with whom your agent will be interfacing. Walk through the real estate process and identify to the agent whether your staff or vendor(s) will handle the particular task or if you would like the agent to handle it. This applies to communicating with occupant(s), rekeying, property trash out, personal property disposition, sales clean, yard cleanup, and ongoing yard maintenance. Let the agent know if you have preferred vendors you would like the agent to use or if you need the agent to refer a vendor. Open communication about your expectations will be appreciated by your agent and result in a positive and productive working relationship.

If the property is occupied, inform your agent of the occupant's contact information if you have it. Alternatively, you can ask your agent to visit the property and contact the occupant(s) by door knocking. If an occupant is no longer paying rent or paying under-market rent, your agent should be able to facilitate a Cash for Keys or Voluntary Buyout Agreement. Facilitating this type of arrangement ultimately serves as the most cost-effective method, as the occupant does not feel threatened, and is cooperative, most of the time. This saves time, and money, on eviction and potential litigation.

If a property management company is handling the real estate asset, provide your agent with their contact information. Let your agent know which vendor you would like to use for escrow and title services, and update your agent on the referee's valuation status.

Marketing Strategy Expectations

Your agent should identify in the valuation report, otherwise known as the Comparative Market Analysis (CMA), Broker's Price Opinion (BPO), or BOV (Broker Opinion of Value), what the property's As-Is value is. Suppose you or your clients are interested in exploring renovating the property to maximize the return on the property's sale. In that case, you can request that your agent complete a cost/benefit analysis by identifying comparables of the property that are in newly renovated condition.

Suppose the repair strategy is selected based on your agent's analysis. In that case, you should conduct your due diligence by ordering inspection report(s) that allow you to determine the current condition of the property and identify the repairs required to be made and their actual costs. Types of inspection reports include general home, mold and moisture, sewer line, and chimney. The general home inspection report will identify any other areas of concern, for example, if the general home inspector suspects foundation issues, a specialized foundation inspector will be referred for a more thorough inspection. For the mold and moisture inspection, the inspector uses an infrared camera and moisture meter to detect moisture behind walls, ceilings, and floors. The inspector pays special attention to plumbing areas and takes readings under sinks and the places where mold is most commonly found. Conducting these inspections before launching a renovation project is critical since it will affect the bottom line of the sale's return. It will alleviate the seller's concern of finding mold during the renovation process, for example, behind the bathroom cabinets, and then worrying about the extra cost to mitigate. These reports should be provided to the bidding vendor to determine the cost to renovate.

Suppose it is determined that the repair cost is too high after the inspections have been completed, given the projected return on the sale. In that case, you and your client may decide not to proceed with a renovation and sell the property in As-Is condition. All of the inspection reports will be shared with all buyers in advance of offer negotiations and acceptance.

For example, if it is determined that the property has foundation issues, it does not make sense to renovate the property and leave the foundation issues unrepaired. Renovating a property is a marketing strategy that targets owner-occupant buyers, and disclosing to owner-occupant buyers that the property is renovated, and has foundation issues, will turn away these types of buyers.

Selling a property in As-Is condition refers to the state that the property is in when an offer is accepted. This strategy is preferred when the cost to repair a real estate asset does not justify renovating based on the anticipated return. An As-Is property typically attracts investor buyers. However, savvy owner-occupants who are not afraid to renovate do show interest on many occasions.

The seller is still obligated to ensure that any state and local laws are adhered to before the close of escrow, such as making retrofitting repairs and delivering a city inspection report to the buyer before closing escrow. These requirements must be adhered to, even when the property is being sold in As-Is condition.

Pricing Expectations

You should review your agent's CMA/BPO/BOV for accuracy. Ensure that the comparable properties selected are relevant in terms of sold date, distance from the subject property, interior square footage, and bed/bath count. Pricing the CMA/BPO/BOV competitively initially will generate the highest return on the sale. Competitive pricing creates demand and desire, and in turn, a multiple offer situation creates pressure for buyers and encourages them to offer as much as they can.

Your agent should recommend the listing price. If you insist that the property is priced higher, your agent should comply by listing at that price, but propose to monitor the market and report back every couple of weeks. Price reductions could be made accordingly, to the point where there is a multiple offer situation. Once there is a multiple offer situation, all buyers should be countered with a "highest and best" request and a deadline for a response should be set. If your agent receives calls from buyer's agents asking how much their buyer client should offer, the response should be to offer as much as they can so they don't regret it if they lose the property.

If there is very little activity after two weeks, your agent should reach out to you and request a price reduction. Comparables should be provided to you so you have data to support this change. This should be an ongoing process and should continue every two weeks until there is an offer. Once there is one offer, if it is below the list price, your agent may suggest to counter at the listing price rather than accept the offer. The buyer will most likely not come up in price, given it is the only offer on the table, and there is no competition with other buyers. In this case, your agent should reduce the property's list price to the same price that the buyer is offering. Why not open up the property to the market at the same price, see if there are any other takers, and create a multiple offer situation? Time and time again, this strategy proves to be effective. A multiple offer situation is created. Demand and excitement generate the highest possible price for the property and sell for the price that the market can bear.

Ultimately, it is best to price a property competitively from the outset, based on facts, so time is not wasted on price reductions.

Scope Expectations

It would be best to discuss the project's scope to get the property ready for market.   You can review the list below with your team and your agent and decide who will handle it, and also discuss if any vendor referrals are needed:

- Rekey
- Utilities
- Personal Property Inventory and Disposition
- Trash out
- Sales Clean and Disinfecting
- Yard Cleanup and Maintenance
- Pool/Spa Cleanup and Maintenance
- Winterization
- Snow Removal
- Repairs and Renovations
- Local and State Retrofitting

Reporting Expectations

There should be open communication between you, your agent, the attorney on this case, the eviction attorney (if an eviction is being pursued), and escrow and title throughout the real estate sale process.

If the property is occupied, your agent should update you on discussions had with the occupant(s). If an eviction is being pursued, your agent should report to you and the eviction attorney when access is denied by the occupant(s). This information will be useful to the eviction attorney and documented as part of the case.

If the property is vacant, your agent should provide you with interior photos and a repair list with estimated costs for repair. The referee does a drive-by of the property and does not enter to inspect. Your agent's feedback on the property's interior condition will impact the appraised value set by the referee.

In a full authority situation where court confirmation is not required, your agent reports to the attorney when there is an accepted offer so that the attorney can issue a Notice of Proposed Action.

In a limited authority situation where court confirmation is required, inform your agent of the referee's appraised value, so the agent is aware of the minimum acceptable offer and ensures that the offer accepted subject to court confirmation is at least 90% of the appraised value. Once there is an accepted offer, your agent should inform you or the attorney so that a court hearing can be scheduled, and the escrow and title vendors should be informed as well. The attorney must also publish the Notice of Sale in a newspaper published in the county in which the real property is located.

Your agent will instruct the buyer on where to send the earnest money deposit, as well as the amount and to whom it should be payable, and you should communicate with your agent once you have received it.

Once escrow opens, your agent should update you throughout the escrow process, including but not limited to:

- Scheduled date of inspections (on sales not requiring court confirmation)
- Removal of contingencies (on sales not requiring court confirmation)
- Final walkthrough
- One week before the closing date, a closing readiness update should be provided. Your agent should check in

with all parties: escrow, buyer's agent, and you, to ensure that everyone is ready to close in one week and then provide an update to all. This procedure allows all parties to prioritize to ensure they can close on time.

Chapter 3: Pre-Marketing Strategies

Chapter Overview

The pre-marketing strategy that you select for the property that you are selling has a significant impact on the type of return you will achieve for your client. Understanding the various strategies that may be used for residential and commercial vacant and occupied properties and determining which strategy to use, is critical in the ultimate successful sale of the property.

Chapter Outline

Understanding the Current Situation

Deciding on the Marketing Strategy for Vacant Units

- Renovate and Sell Vacant
- Renovate and Lease Before Selling
- Sell As-Is Vacant
- Lease and Sell As-Is

Deciding on the Marketing Strategy for Occupied Units

- Selling Occupied As-Is
- Renovate and Increase Rents
- Add Tenant(s)
- Remove Tenant(s), Sell As-Is
- Remove Tenant(s), Lease As-Is
- Remove Tenant(s), Renovate, and Sell

Introduction

Your goal in determining your property's pre-marketing strategy is to provide your client with the highest return on the sale of the property being sold.

Understanding the Current Situation

As a first step, you should determine the current situation by conducting your due diligence to identify if the property is vacant, partially vacant, or occupied. If occupied, are the occupants paying rent? Are they paying under-market rents? What is the condition of the exterior of the property? What is the condition of the interior?

If you wish, your agent can assist you with determining answers to all of the questions above. Your agent can call the occupants, and if you do not have the contact information for the occupant(s), your agent can visit the property and speak with the occupant(s) or post a notice on the door to call the agent.

Suppose the property that needs to be sold is a multi-family property, and the rents being paid are unknown. In that case, your agent can visit the property and request an Estoppel Certificate to be completed by the occupant(s) in all of the units.

Deciding on the Marketing Strategy

Vacant Units

Let's take a look at the strategies available for vacant units:

- Renovate and Sell Vacant
- Renovate and Lease Before Selling
- Sell As-Is Vacant
- Lease and Sell As-Is

These strategies are discussed in detail below.

Renovate and Sell Vacant

Suppose the property being sold is a residential or multi-family property and is not in move-in condition. In that case, your agent can proceed with a cost/benefit analysis to renovate the property and add value to maximize the return on the property's sale. If it makes sense to renovate, your agent should proceed with inspections that will help identify which repairs should be made and then work with your agent's team of preferred vendors to bid on the project and proceed with the renovation project. Your agent should oversee the vendors' work.

If the property is a non-residential commercial property, the renovation would consist of white-box construction: a partially finished commercial space delivered to a landlord or tenant. There is a bare finished ceiling, concrete floors sufficient for most flooring types, white sheet-rocked walls, and essential HVAC. The interior walls are not included, other than the code required restrooms, nor does it include: wall coverings, paint, flooring, plumbing fixtures, or upgraded electrical fixtures. A white box build-out is ready for TI's (tenant improvements) to be completed once a lease agreement has been negotiated and executed.

Renovate and Lease Before Selling

If the property is a vacant single-family residence, or multi-unit residential property (2-4 units), leasing it during the process may serve to be beneficial. By leasing the property, you will be generating income that will pay the bills such as property taxes, insurance, the mortgage payment, as well as repairs and maintenance.

If the property, on the other hand, is a commercial property that is vacant or does not have full occupancy, such as a standalone retail building, industrial, or multi-family, leasing the property, so there is a 100 percent occupancy rate or close to it, will yield your client the highest sales price once sold.

For example, for a retail or industrial property, a standalone building, by signing a leasing contract with a national tenant, you increase the property's market value drastically. These single-tenant, triple net properties are leased to one tenant, and the tenant pays for property taxes, property insurance, and the CAM (Common Area Maintenance) fees. A single tenant lease is long-term, typically 10-25 years. A national tenant has a national footprint and is widely known by the general public. Having a long-term leasing contract with a national tenant increases the net operating income, which increases the capitalization rate and the market value of the property. The renovation effort on these types of properties would consist of white boxing to allow each tenant to customize their own space. See details on white boxing in the section above, "Renovate and Sell Vacant".

For multi-family properties, it is best to attract the highest quality tenant possible, so rents can be increased, thus increasing the net operating income. To achieve that, common areas should be cleaned up and renovated: fresh paint, new flooring, etc. Making simple improvements to the units such as modern flooring, fresh paint, and new kitchen cabinets and appliances, including a dishwasher, will attract tenants willing to pay higher rents. By increasing the net operating income, the capitalization rate is increased, and therefore the current market value of the property increases.

Sell As-Is Vacant

Suppose the property being sold is a vacant residential or commercial property not in move-in condition. The cost/benefit analysis indicates that it does not make sense to renovate, or there is no time to renovate and lease given the timeline. In that case, the property should be sold As-Is and vacant. Also, if the property is in move-in condition already, it would make sense to sell it As-Is. To maximize the sale's return, the property should be clear of personal property and trash, and a thorough deep sales clean should be completed, so the property smells good and looks clean and is pleasant to tour.

Lease and Sell As-Is

Both residential and commercial real property could increase in value by occupying them with tenants paying market rents. If the property is in reasonable condition, it can be leased at market rents without renovating it, and this will allow you to sell it to an investor. This is especially beneficial for commercial properties such as retail, industrial, and multi-family. The property's market value depends on the cap rate, which increases with increased net operating income.

Occupied Units

If the property you need to sell is occupied, the first steps are to identify if rents are being paid by the tenants and the amounts being paid. If you do not have copies of the leases, you or your agent can request that each tenant complete and sign an Estoppel Certificate (EC).

If you have leases, it is still a good idea to have each tenant complete and sign the EC, so that it is clear what was previously agreed to verbally between tenant and landlord. This form, once completed, describes the nature of the relationship between the occupant and the landlord, and will be provided to any prospective buyer(s), giving them notice about the rights and privileges that the existing tenants have. The certificate requests basic information such as the current tenants' name, a copy of the lease and date of the lease, monthly rent being paid, and other lease terms. It also allows the tenant to specify who is to pay for utilities, tenant or landlord.

The tenant is not required to complete it. However, it is in the tenant's best interest to complete it and document any prior oral agreements that are contradictory or not addressed, in the lease, to protect their rights. Examples of prior oral agreements include permission to have a pet, permission to sublease or have a roommate, or free use of a storage area or a parking spot.

The lease may include a provision indicating that the tenant must complete an EC within a certain period of time, in which case, the tenant's refusal to cooperate would result in a breach of the lease contract. Per CA Civil Code 2079.16, your real estate agent has a duty to provide buyers with all estoppel certificates in their possession.

Once the rental amounts being paid by each tenant have been established, work with your agent to strategize on getting the highest return on the sale of the property. If the rents being paid are under market value, consider increasing rents or getting the units vacant. If no rents are being paid, consider getting these units vacant. You can get the units vacant by offering CFK (Cash for Keys), otherwise known as a Tenant Buyout Agreement, Relocation Assistance, or a Voluntary Buyout. If the tenants are not paying rent or are not adhering to the lease terms, it would be considered an at-fault eviction. It would allow you to negotiate the CFK amount with the tenants and not adhere to the local laws requiring specific CFK amounts.

Determine if the property falls within the California State Rent Control Assembly Bill 1482, and if so, adhere to those regulations. If considering increasing rents, the housing department can advise on amounts that adhere to local laws.

It is possible to conduct a "without cause" eviction in rent-controlled properties by offering CFK in these situations:

- Rents are under market value.
- The landlord wishes to remodel/renovate.
- The landlord has purchased a new rental property and wants to rent to tenants they have personally screened and approved.

If the tenant accepts and moves out, the landlord can increase rents to as high as the next tenant agrees to pay. The rent control increase limits would now apply to this new higher amount. It is crucial to adhere to the required relocation amounts offered to tenants and the disclosure requirements in these situations, as mandated by local laws.

These are six strategies that may be used to maximize the return on the sale of occupied properties:

- Selling Occupied As-Is
- Renovate and Increase Rents
- Add Tenant(s)
- Remove Tenant(s), Sell As-Is
- Remove Tenant(s), Lease As-Is Before Sale
- Remove Tenant(s), Renovate, and Sell

These strategies are discussed in detail below.

Selling Occupied As Is

Selling an occupied residential or multi-family property occupied where rents being paid are under-market value or no rents are being paid will require you to sell the property to an investor who will purchase at a discount. Sometimes this makes sense since the timeline is short, and there is no cooperation from the tenant(s) in accepting CFK, and the eviction process is too long. The investor will need to negotiate CFK with the occupant or evict the occupant. A sophisticated investor will have a relationship with an evictions attorney and have already consulted with the attorney before submitting an offer to determine the course of action available to get the property vacant once the buyer has purchased the property and the costs involved. The investor will have sufficient funds to buy the property and pay the eviction attorney and carrying costs for the duration of time the property is occupied.

The unsophisticated buyer does not take the time to consult with an eviction attorney. This type of buyer delays submitting the earnest money deposit into escrow to buy time to knock on the door, let the occupant know that he is the new owner and negotiate the CFK offer. If the buyer does not get the results he wants, the buyer cancels the transaction before depositing the earnest money deposit into escrow and thus wasting your time. Your agent must conduct the proper vetting of buyers and identify the qualified sophisticated investors capable of purchasing occupied properties, which will save you and your client time and money.

Renovate and Increase Rents

Renovating a multi-family property allows you to increase rents. For example, adding a dishwasher to each occupied unit can justify increasing rent in a multi-family property. Increasing the net operating income (NOI) allows you to list the property at a higher list price and get the highest return on your client's sale. Note that this is not a feasible strategy for properties located in rent-controlled areas.

Add Tenant(s)

The same general principles apply to other types of commercial properties, such as shopping centers. The goal is to increase the NOI so the property's value is increased. Increasing NOI for a shopping center, for example, means placing higher quality tenants or national tenants either in vacant units or in units where tenants are not paying their rent. National and higher quality tenants will likely have longer-term contracts and may attract other quality tenants. Increasing the NOI with the addition of tenants, in turn, increases the property's market value.

Remove Tenant(s), Sell As-Is

If the tenant(s) are not adding value to the property, for example, they are not paying rent or paying under-market rents, it makes sense to get the property vacant. If the cost/benefit analysis indicates that it does not make sense to renovate, sell the property in As-Is condition once it becomes vacant to maximize the sale's return.

Offering CFK is considered a voluntary buyout. The occupant agrees to move out in exchange for compensation. Depending on where the property is located and the type of property, there may be specific CFK requirements. For example, if a property is located within City of Los Angeles and the property is a multi-unit (2 or more units) and is built before October 1, 1978, the landlord must provide tenant an RSO (Rent Stabilization Ordinance) Disclosure defining tenant's rights, along with the CFK contract. This should be submitted to the City of Los Angeles Housing Department within 60 days of signing the fully executed contract. However, if the property is a single-family residence, these requirements do not apply, and only the California state law civil code for tenant's rights and landlord's responsibilities apply. Every city has specific requirements, and the proper due diligence must be conducted to determine the procedural requirements for CFK. Your agent should check to see which city the property is located in, or if it is situated in an unincorporated area of a county, and then determine their CFK requirements. If the property is located in an area with rent control, there may be specific disclosure requirements.

Your agent should possess the ability and skill to reach out to each occupant and listen to their stories and understand their circumstances and needs. The goal is for your agent to establish a rapport and negotiate a fair CFK amount, so the occupant is motivated to move out by the selected move-out date. Perhaps the occupant was the decedent's caretaker and could not find or qualify for a new residence to relocate. Another scenario may be occupants who used to be rent-paying tenants, but they can no longer pay rent due to unfortunate circumstances. CFK should be the initial attempt at getting the property vacant before considering an eviction. It saves time and money and does not create the tension and upset that filing an unlawful detainer (eviction) creates. CFK generates greater cooperation, and has shown to generate much success in getting occupants to move out on time and leaving the property clean, as agreed. When the occupant's request is not a reasonable one or the occupant refuses to vacate the property despite the offering of CFK, the owner may resort to evicting the occupant.

Remove Tenant(s), Lease As-Is Before Sale

We already discussed how to get a property vacant: CFK, otherwise known as a Voluntary Buyout, or Relocation Assistance, which serves to be the most cost-effective majority of the time. If there is an at-fault just cause for an eviction, and the tenant is not cooperating with CFK, an eviction attorney should be engaged to proceed with an unlawful detainer. A no-fault just cause eviction requires that the landlord pay a relocation fee to the tenant(s). If the tenant(s) are paying under-market rents for a commercial property in good condition, it makes sense to get the property vacant, lease it, and then sell it.

Remove Tenant(s), Renovate, and Sell

If the tenant(s) are not paying rent, removing the tenants can be accomplished using CFK, as we have learned. If the property is a residential property that has been left by the tenant(s) in poor condition, renovate it if the cost/benefit analysis makes sense. If it is a commercial property, white box it to get a higher sales price. This strategy applies if there is insufficient time to lease the commercial property given the timeline.

Chapter 4: Cash for Keys Process and Agreement

Chapter Overview

Cash for Keys is a useful tool used to get an occupied property to become vacant and avoid eviction. Your agent must conduct the proper due diligence to prevent legal liability. It takes patience and empathy to work with the occupant and arrive at an agreement that is mutually beneficial to all parties. Your agent should work with the occupant to ensure the occupant moves out on time, as agreed to, and that the property is left without personal property or trash to prevent additional costs to the estate.

Chapter Outline

Introduction

The Cash for Keys Process

      Due Diligence: Location and Local Requirements

      Determining Initial CFK Terms

      Making Contact with Occupant

      Negotiating Relocation/CFK Terms

      Executing the Cash for Keys Agreement

      Property Inspection and Delivery of Payment

The Cash for Keys Agreement

Introduction

Cash for Keys is an agreement between the owner of a property and a tenant to move out on an agreed-upon date in exchange for an agreed-upon sum of money. It is also known as a Relocation Agreement, Tenant Buyout Agreement, or a Voluntary Buyout. This is a way to convince a tenant to move out of a property and is an alternative to an eviction proceeding.

Experienced agents handle Cash for Keys for their clients as a first step to try to avoid evictions. Per the CFK agreement, the property must be delivered free of trash and personal property, both inside the property, the exterior, and any detached structures such as sheds and/or garages.

There are many success stories where a mere $5,000 was motivating enough to a non-paying tenant to move out in 45 days and leave the property in broom swept condition. That is an excellent deal for the seller, as we all know how expensive trash outs can be and the cost of an eviction and possible litigation.

The Cash for Keys Process

An experienced agent can handle the entire process - from reaching out to the occupant, getting the C.A.R. CFK agreement negotiated and executed, meeting the occupant at the property to conduct a walkthrough, and providing the occupant with payment.

Due Diligence: Location and Local Requirements (Step 1)

Your agent should first identify if the property is located within city limits or a county's jurisdiction. Your agent's due diligence consists of calling the city or county's housing department to identify if there are specific CFK amount or disclosure requirements and what the process is. An eviction attorney can confirm the requirements related to the relocation amounts and disclosure requirements that may pertain to local laws, depending on whether the occupants are at fault or no-fault. Your eviction attorney can also review the Cash for Keys Agreement to ensure all required language has been included, including releasing all known and unknown claims.

Determining Initial CFK Terms (Step 2)

After conducting the proper due diligence, you and your agent should discuss the CFK terms to offer to the occupant. If local laws require that you offer a specific CFK amount, this amount should be provided to the occupant. If the offer amount is at the owner's discretion, your agent should take a graduated approach. For example, start with offering the occupant $2,500, and you can negotiate up to $8,000 to leave in a timeframe between 30-45 days. The shorter timeframe to move out, the better, and the lower the offer amount, the better. Your agent should act strategically to negotiate the best terms on your behalf.

Making Contact with Occupant (Step 3)

If you have the occupant's contact information, provide it to your agent to call and establish rapport and understand the occupant's needs and situation. Suppose you do not have the occupant's contact information. In that case, your agent should visit the property and knock on the door. If there is no answer, your agent should leave a notice taped to the front door that includes the following information:

- Agent's contact information, indicating that the agent would like to discuss possible financial relocation assistance to help cover moving costs.
- To be eligible for this assistance, the occupant must vacate the property within the agreed time frame and leave it in broom-swept condition.
- Certain restrictions apply.
- Indicate that occupant should reach out to your agent within five business days to discuss the options. The deadline to respond creates a sense of urgency.

Negotiating Relocation/CFK Terms (Step 4)

Once your agent has made contact with the occupant, your agent should take the time to listen to the occupant's story and understand the situation and needs of the occupants. Your agent should proceed by educating the occupant on the terms and requirements of the CFK agreement. The occupant's obligations should be discussed, including that the property must be delivered in broom swept condition with no personal property or trash left behind. The interior and exterior of the property must be maintained in good condition. Your agent should negotiate a move-out date in exchange for a payment to be made by the property owner.

Executing the Cash for Keys Agreement (Step 5)

Once an agreement on the move-out date and CFK payment amount has been reached, your agent should contact you for final approval, and you and the occupant should sign the contract. Suppose the property is located in an area that requires specific disclosure requirements per local law. In that case, your agent should provide those disclosures at the appropriate time to the occupant for review and execution.

Property Inspection and Delivery of Payment (Step 6)

Your agent should arrange with the occupant a date and time to meet at the property for a property inspection and delivery of the CFK check. This will be the move-out date. Your agent should remind the occupant once again, a day or two before the move-out date, that if the property's interior and exterior are not in broom-swept condition, the occupant will not receive the CFK payment.

On the move-out date, your agent should conduct a walkthrough of the property's interior and exterior, check to make sure the property has been maintained in good condition, and no trash or personal property left behind. Your agent should open closet doors, kitchen cabinet doors, and appliances such as the refrigerator to ensure nothing is left behind. The garage's interior should also be inspected, and the interior of any cabinets or closets in the garage should be inspected as well. In the property's exterior, your agent should check any sheds or storage units to ensure they are free from debris, trash, or personal property.

Suppose your agent finds that the property is not yet ready. In that case, your agent should discuss this with the occupant and allow the occupant an opportunity to remedy the situation and have it in compliance later in the day. Your agent should schedule to return to the property later in the day for a reinspection. Once the property complies with the terms of the CFK agreement and the occupant provides your agent with all keys and remotes, your agent should take complete photos showing the property is in broom-swept condition and give the occupant the CFK payment.

It does take some time to establish rapport with the occupant. It takes time to listen to their story, exhibit empathy for their situations, and share this great opportunity and its benefits with them. A real estate agent with the right personality traits will be able to skillfully negotiate a Cash for Keys on your behalf and save your client time and money. Unfortunately, some occupants will not vacate the property until there is a court order and willfully continue to live in the property at no cost until such time. In these cases, you would proceed with the eviction process.

The Cash for Keys Agreement

The occupant must sign a Cash for Keys Agreement, and the contract specifies the following:

- The move-out date and the CFK offer amount.
- That the occupant will not damage the property.

- That the cost to repair any damage, along with the cost of any unpaid utility bills, will be deducted from the CFK offer amount.
- That the occupant(s) will leave the property clean, both interior and exterior, in broom-swept condition on the move-out date.
- That you have the right to bring an unlawful detainer (eviction) action against any occupant who does not vacate after the move-out date.
- That the occupant agrees to cooperate and will allow access for showings to prospective buyer(s) or tenant(s).
- That occupant is signing a waiver of rights to any minimum notice to end the occupancy, which the owner usually provides.
- All adult occupants must sign the agreement, and by signing, each occupant holds harmless and releases the owner, its agents, successors, and assigns from any action related to the property.

This is a voluntary agreement with the occupant moving out on their own negotiated terms and is less risky than pursuing an eviction action. A CFK agreement within reason is better than an eviction. It allows you to reduce the risk of litigation and creates a better upside. Sometimes the negotiated terms may be waiving the payment of two months of rent and returning a deposit, along with a CFK payment. For example, a $3,000 deposit may be returned to the occupant, and a $5,000 payment may be made to the occupant.

This may upset you or your clients - the heirs or beneficiaries. However, this should not be an emotional decision. It should be handled as a real estate investment matter. It will be more cost-effective to offer those CFK terms than to pay the cost of an eviction and possible litigation.

Your CFK agreement should include a complete release of claims clause, which consists of those claims that the occupant may not know about to protect you. For example, the occupant who has resided in an unpermitted, illegal unit may come back to you after moving out with a claim that you rented them an illegal unit.

Getting an eviction attorney to reach out to the occupant and negotiate the CFK will create additional costs. Not only will you be paying for the time the attorney spends speaking with the occupant(s), but the occupant may hire an attorney specializing in tenant protection to act on their behalf and speak with your attorney. Then the requested CFK amount will be significantly higher, as it will be a settlement.

The eviction attorney should be consulted to confirm the local requirements, given the property's location. The eviction attorney should advise on any disclosure requirements. For example, Los Angeles county has specific disclosure requirements on relocation assistance being offered to tenants. Those agreements must be delivered to the occupants at the right time, as stipulated by local laws. There are also relocation amount requirements that your eviction attorney may advise on if the tenant is at no fault. If the tenant is at fault, say, for not paying rent, the CFK amount is negotiable and not a requirement set by local laws. If this is your first CFK agreement, or if your agent is not highly experienced with CFK, the eviction attorney should also review the CFK agreement and advise on verbiage to ensure a complete release of all claims is included appropriately.

Chapter 5: The Eviction Process

Chapter Overview

The eviction process can be either straightforward or lengthy, depending on whether the occupant responds to the complaint and whether the occupant requests a jury trial. You must seek the assistance of an attorney specializing in evictions to ensure the proper procedures are adhered to, and delays are prevented. Once the occupant has vacated the property, any personal property left behind must be cataloged. The appropriate notices must be issued to allow for the owner of the personal property to reclaim it.

Chapter Outline

Introduction

Summary of the Eviction Process

Issuing Notice to Terminate Tenancy

    Giving Notice for At Fault

    Giving Notice for No-Fault

Filing an Unlawful Detainer Summons and Complaint

Tenant Responds to Complaint?

Court Hearing

Set for Trial, Settlement Conference, and Trial

Landlord Favored?

Tenant Files Demand for Jury Trial

Landlord Files for Default Judgement

Writ of Possession Issued

Sheriff Posts Notice

Sheriff Lockout

Documenting Personal Property Left Behind

Delivering Notice of Right to Reclaim Abandoned Personal Property

Storing Abandoned Property

Personal Property Claimed?

Releasing Abandoned Property

Conducting a Public Sale of Personal Property

Handling Sale Proceeds

Handling Abandoned Vehicles

Handling Squatters

Introduction

California eviction laws mandate that landlords/property owners use the court statutory process to evict a tenant and cannot perform a "self-help eviction," which is considered an illegal eviction. Examples of self-help methods include: ordering the tenant to leave, locking out the tenant by changing the locks, removing personal property of the tenant from the property, stop paying the utility bills so utilities are turned off, and any other type of threatening or harassing actions towards the tenant. This type of behavior will most likely lead to the landlord's liability as the tenant may sue the landlord for trespassing, intentional infliction of emotional distress, or wrongful eviction.

The California eviction process is referred to as an unlawful detainer lawsuit. It is a summary court procedure, meaning the court process moves along quickly, giving a tenant a brief period to respond after being served with the summons and complaint. In regular times, a hearing would take place within approximately three weeks after a request has been made to set the case for trial.

You must consult with an eviction attorney at the beginning of the process to ensure the proper notices are issued promptly and correctly. Securing the services of an attorney who specializes in evictions is essential to ensure a successful outcome. Eviction laws rapidly change at the federal, state, county, and city levels, and it is crucial to have a specialized attorney who is up to date with all laws and regulations.

A tenant may decide to fight the eviction and claim that the landlord made procedural mistakes such as improperly serving a notice or waiting long enough before filing the eviction lawsuit. Other defenses include that the landlord did not maintain the property, or discriminated against the tenant.

Summary of the Eviction Process

An eviction is executed (effectuated) under the California court order known as an unlawful detainer judgment. The general process includes serving the occupant(s) with a written 3, 30, 60, or 90-day notice to terminate the tenancy. The landlord files an Unlawful Detainer Summons and Complaint and serves the occupant. If the occupant does not respond, which is the most straightforward eviction path, the landlord prepares a Default Judgment and then secures a Writ of Possession. A sheriff's notice is then issued, and a sheriff's lockout follows. If the tenant files a Demurrer or Motion to Strike or a Motion to Quash Service of Summons, a hearing is scheduled, and if the tenant loses, the tenant may request a Jury Trial. The tenant may also respond to the UD Summons and Complaint with a Demand for Jury Trial, in which case a Request to Set Case for Trial would be issued. Then a Settlement Conference would be scheduled. A trial would take place for 1-4 days, and if the occupant loses, a sheriff's notice would be issued, followed by the sheriff's lockout.

The risks involved in pursuing an unlawful detainer judgment is that the occupant may take the lengthier route of the eviction process and respond to the landlord's filing of the Unlawful Detainer Summons and Complaint with a Demand for Jury Trial and retain a tenants' rights attorney for representation. This will drag the eviction process longer. Most of the time, a settlement is negotiated.

The steps of the process are elaborated on in the ensuing paragraphs.

Issuing Notice to Terminate Tenancy (Step 1)

A landlord can terminate the tenancy with or without cause. However, if there is rent control, a reason is required to terminate the tenancy.

Giving Notice for At Fault

At-fault eviction causes include a tenant's non-payment of rent or late payment of rent, other lease violations, being the cause of a nuisance, damaging the property, and reducing its value.

To legally terminate the tenancy, a landlord must first give written notice. In areas where there is rent control, there are additional rules required to terminate a tenancy.

The types of notices include a Three-Day Notice to Pay Rent, a Three-Day Notice to Cure, or a Three-Day Unconditional Quit Notice. The California Association of Realtors has forms available to its Realtors:

- Form PRQ (Notice to Pay Rent or Quit) - gives the tenant three days to either pay rent and stay or leave.
- Form PCQ (Notice to Perform Covenant (Cure) or Quit) – gives the tenant three days to perform a covenant of the lease, such as

ensuring there are no pets on the premises and stay or leave.
- Form NTQ (Notice to Quit) – for severe or incurable violations of the lease, this is an unconditional notice specifying to get out within three days.

Serving the Three-Day Notice

The notice can be delivered in person, and if the tenant is not available, it should be posted at the property, and two date-stamped photos should be taken of the posting, one from a distance and the other up close. The day of service is counted as day zero, and the next day after the day of service is counted as day one. Weekends, legal holidays, and "court holidays" (when courts are closed) are not counted as part of the three days.

Accepting Rent within the Three-Day Notice Period

If the tenant offers to pay the full rent amount within three days of receiving the Notice to Pay Rent or Quit, you must accept the payment, and the tenant may remain in possession.

However, if the tenant offers partial payment, you can refuse to accept and continue the eviction process. Acceptance of partial payment can invalidate a three-day notice. This rule relates to residential tenancies, not commercial tenancies where partial payments might be acceptable under certain circumstances.

If the rent is not paid within three days or if you refuse to accept a partial payment, and the tenant does not vacate the premises, you can then file an unlawful detainer action to terminate the tenancy and recover possession.

Giving Notice for No-Fault

A no-fault eviction refers to a situation where the landlord does not wish to renew a tenant lease. On month-to-month leases, if the landlord chooses not to renew a lease and wants to terminate the tenant's lease, the landlord must notify the tenant that the tenancy will expire at the end of the notice period and the tenant must move out by that time. The C.A.R. form NTT (Notice of Termination of Tenancy) may be used for this purpose.

30-day Notice

If a tenant has lived in the property for under a year, a 30-day notice is usually required.

60-day Notice

For a tenant who has lived in the property for over a year, a 60-day notice is required.

Exception to the 60-day Notice

There is an exception when a month-to-month tenant has lived in the property for more than a year. The seller need only give a 30-day notice to terminate if ALL six of the following criteria are met:

1. The seller has entered into a contract to sell the property to a natural person(s).
2. The purchaser intends to reside in the premises for at least one year following the termination of tenancy.
3. The landlord has established an escrow with an escrow company licensed by the Department of Corporations.
4. The escrow was opened 120 days or less before the delivery of the notice.
5. The title to the premises is separately alienable from any other dwelling unit (i.e., a single-family unit or condominium).
6. The tenant has not previously been given a notice of termination of tenancy.

As long as all six of the above criteria have been met, then even a month-to-month tenant that has been in the property for more than a year may be given a 30-day notice to terminate the tenancy. See section three of C.A.R. form NTT.

On fixed-term leases that are for periods longer than month-to-month, the landlord must wait for the lease term to end and is not required to provide a notice to move out at the end of the term unless the terms of the lease state that it is necessary.

A tenant's fixed-term lease expires, but the tenant refuses to move

If the tenant's fixed-term lease expires, but the tenant refuses to move out, the owner can proceed with the unlawful detainer action. The lease agreement provides the tenant with notice of termination of the tenancy. While formal notice may not be required if the requirement for such is not specified in the lease, you should, however, inform the tenant in writing at least 30 days before their lease expiration date and indicate that there will be no renewal of the lease or any continuation of the tenancy. Your agent can use C.A.R.'s Sample Letter titled "Lease Expiration Letter".

When the tenant is under the Section 8 program, or rent control, or is pursuant to applicable "foreclosed-tenant" statutes, the owner may have to provide a 90-day notice.

Filing an Unlawful Detainer Summons and Complaint (Step 2)

After serving the tenant with notice, you must allow the appropriate notice period (i.e., 3, 30, 60, or 90 days) to pass to allow the tenant to cure the violation or vacate the premises within the specified time period. If the tenant refuses, then the landlord proceeds with filing an unlawful detainer (UD) action in court.

The landlord files a complaint with the court, which includes facts that justify the eviction, along with a request for back rent and damages, if applicable. The landlord must serve the tenant with the complaint and a summons, which is the document informing the tenant of the lawsuit.

In residential eviction complaints, specific documents should be attached to the UD complaint: a copy of the lease agreement, the notice of termination, and a Proof of Service indicating how the notice of termination was served. The complaint must also be "verified" (signed by the property owner under penalty of perjury).

Tenant Responds to Complaint? (Decision Point D1)

After the tenant is personally served with the UD complaint, the tenant has five days to respond. Other forms of service may dictate different allowable response periods. The tenant may respond by submitting a defense, indicating that rent was not paid to make necessary repairs that the landlord refused to make. Or, the tenant may deny the allegations being made.

The tenant may file a demand for a jury trial, demurrer, motion to strike, or motion to quash service of summons.

Court Hearing (Step 3a)

If the tenant responds to the complaint, challenging the eviction, with a demurrer, a motion to strike, or a motion to quash service of summons, a court hearing date is set for the contested eviction; usually, three weeks after the answer is filed.

Set for Trial, Settlement Conference, and Trial (Step 3b)

Suppose the tenant responds to the complaint with a demand for a jury trial. In that case, a request to set the case for trial is made, and a settlement conference is scheduled. Then a trial takes place. If the landlord is favored in trial, the tenant can appeal up to the California Supreme Court.

Also, a tenant may demand a jury trial after a landlord is favored at a court hearing.

Landlord Favored? (Decision Point D2)

At the court hearing, if the judge favors the landlord, the judge will sign an Order granting possession or a monetary award for damages, after which a writ of possession directing the sheriff to proceed with eviction can be issued. If the landlord is not favored, the tenant stays in possession.

Tenant Files Demand for Jury Trial (Decision Point D3)

The tenant may file a demand for a jury trial if the landlord is favored after the court hearing, which will trigger a request to set a case for trial, a settlement conference is scheduled, and then a trial takes place.

Landlord Files for Default Judgement (Step 3)

If the tenant does not respond to the complaint, the landlord can file for a default judgment immediately without going to court for a hearing. The clerk will then issue a writ of possession, directing the sheriff to eviction. Once issued, a sheriff posts a notice providing the tenant five days to vacate and remove personal property.

Writ of Possession Issued (Step 4)

The court clerk issues a writ of possession if the tenant does not respond to the complaint, and it is an uncontested eviction. It is also issued when the landlord is favored after a court hearing or a jury trial. The writ of possession is then delivered to the sheriff's office to request a lockout.

Sheriff Posts Notice (Step 5)

Once a writ of possession has been obtained, directing the sheriff to proceed with eviction, the sheriff can then post notice giving the tenant a final five days to remove their personal property and vacate the premises.

Sheriff Lockout (Step 6)

If the tenant does not leave within five days, the sheriff will advise the landlord of the date and time of a lockout, during which time the sheriff will physically remove the tenant from the premises and restore possession to the landlord. The landlord will then be allowed to rekey the property.

Documenting Personal Property Left Behind (Step 7)

Once the tenant has vacated the property and the tenancy is terminated, a property walkthrough is required. All personal property that has been left behind must be cataloged: documented and photographed.

Delivering Notice of Right to Reclaim Abandoned Personal Property (Step 8)

You or your agent should provide a written notice informing the tenant that the personal property left behind should be retrieved, or otherwise, it will be sold or disposed of in accordance with the law.

Either you or your agent should deliver the notice to the tenant by email, personal delivery, or first-class mail to the owner's last known address. If the notice is sent by mail to the former tenant, one copy should be sent to the premises vacated by the tenant.

The C.A.R. Sample Letters database includes two letters that may serve as notices to issue to prior residential and commercial tenants:

1. "Notice of Right to Reclaim Abandoned Personal Property (Residential) Letter" (Sample Letter form "APPR")
2. "Abandoned Personal Property (Commercial) Letter " (Sample Letter form "APPC"),

The personal property left behind should be described with as much detail as possible to be identified easily. If there are too many items to fit in the space provided, check the box and attach a separate list of the abandoned property.

The notices include an address where the personal property may be claimed and provide a timeframe for the tenant to claim the personal property. At least 15 days should be provided if the notice is personally delivered and 18 days if the notice is mailed.

Suppose possession of the personal property was granted to the property owner/landlord through a court order and through the execution of a writ of possession by the sheriff. In that case, the above notices are not necessary. Such notice is included as part of the writ of possession served/posted by the Sheriff as part of the eviction process.

For residential properties, if the personal property is believed to be worth less than $700, it can be kept, sold, or destroyed without further notice if it is not reclaimed by the timeframe indicated in the notice. If the value is believed to be $700 or more and not reclaimed, it will be sold at a public sale once the date to claim property given in the notice has lapsed.

For commercial properties, if the personal property is believed to be worth less than either $2,500 or an amount equal to one month's rent for the premises that tenant occupied (whichever is greater), the personal property may be sold, kept, or destroyed without further notice if it is not reclaimed within the timeframe specified. Suppose the personal property is believed to be worth greater than $2,500 or an amount equal to one month's rent (whichever is greater). If the personal property is not reclaimed within the timeframe specified, it will be sold at a public sale after notice of the sale has been given by publication. The tenant has the right to bid on the property at the sale, and, after the personal property is sold and the cost of storage, advertising, and sale is deducted, the remaining money will be paid to the county. The tenant may claim the remaining money at any time within one year from the time the county receives the money.

The notice must comply with the format of the forms presented in the California Civil Code. One notice should be delivered to the tenant and the other to someone other than the tenant if the landlord believes someone else to be the personal property owner.

Storing Abandoned Property (Step 9)

The personal property described in the notice must either be left at the vacated premises or stored in a safe place until the landlord either releases the property to the tenant or rightful owner or, disposes of the property at a public sale.

Personal Property Claimed? (Decision Point D4)

The Notice of Right to Reclaim Abandoned Personal Property provides the address where the personal property may be claimed and includes a deadline to be claimed. If it is not claimed by the deadline provided, depending on the personal property's believed value, it will either be disposed of or sold at a public sale.

Releasing Abandoned Property (Step 10)

A seller may release the property to a former tenant or to any other person the seller reasonably believes to be the property owner as long as the tenant or other owner pays the reasonable storage fees and takes the personal property before the date specified in the written notice.

It is advisable to obtain the person's written declaration claiming to be the owner as to their ownership of the personal property and the basis of their right to reclaim the property. This can protect the landlord if some other claimant later alleges that the property was released to the wrong person. At all times, the owner must remember to act reasonably, making decisions that would answer the question of a judge or jury: "was it reasonable to believe that the person was the owner of the released property?"

Conducting a Public Sale of Personal Property (Step 11)

Once the date to claim property has lapsed, and the personal property is believed to be of value based on the rules indicated earlier, it will be sold at a public sale. The tenant may bid for the item(s) at the sale.

Handling Sale Proceeds

The seller can deduct the reasonable expenses for storage, advertising, and sale from the sale proceeds. If not claimed, the balance must be paid to the county treasury (the county where the sale took place) not more than 30 days after the sale.

The seller may refer the personal property owner to the county treasurer. The personal property owner has one year from the date of sale to file a claim to the treasurer for the balance of the sale proceeds.

Handling Abandoned Vehicles

Almost all municipalities have their own rules, regulations, and ordinances governing the disposition of abandoned vehicles. At all times, all such local statutes and regulations must be reviewed carefully for compliance. You or your agent may reach out to vendors who handle the disposition of abandoned vehicles.

Handling Squatters

You or your agent should contact the local police and seek their assistance. The police should be willing to assist you so long as the squatters concede that they were not given lawful possession. However, if they claim they have a legal right (for example, an alleged oral agreement with the owner), the police might not remove them from the premises. Instead, a court order may be required.

To remove unwilling squatters, you should make a demand that they leave the premises. California law has a provision that may apply to squatters, where, after a five-day notice, the owner can proceed with a forcible detainer action rather than unlawful detainer action.

A forcible detainer action involves different rules and procedures. It may not apply to every squatter situation, where an unlawful detainer or another legal method may be utilized to evict the squatters. You should seek legal advice before deciding the most suitable approach to evict squatters if the police are unwilling to remove them from the property.

Chapter 6: Getting the Property Ready for Market

Chapter Overview

You might want to handle all or some of the tasks discussed in this chapter yourself, have your team handle them, or ask your agent to handle them for you. An experienced agent should help you with any or all of these pre-marketing and ongoing tasks. Your agent should have a network of trusted vendors ready to assist if needed.

Chapter Outline

Introduction

Assigning Responsibilities

Rekeying and Securing the Property

Initial Property Inspection

Personal Property Disposition

Utilities

Initial and Ongoing Maintenance

    Initial and Ongoing Sales Clean

    Initial and Ongoing Yard Maintenance

    Initial and Ongoing Pool Maintenance

    Initial and Ongoing Handling of Safety and Habitability Issues

    Initial Winterization

    Ongoing Snow Removal

    Initial Removal of Distractions

    Ongoing Handling of Emergencies

Renovations

Introduction

Once the property becomes vacant, your agent should visit the property for the initial property inspection and then develop a plan for getting the property ready for market. The basics that should be completed for every property include rekey, trashout, personal property disposition, sales clean, retrofitting, and the following, if applicable: lawn or pool maintenance, winterization, and snow removal. Interior and exterior distractions should also be removed to maximize property value. If your clients are interested in renovating the property before its sale to maximize the return on the sale of the property, discuss this with your agent and proceed with a cost-benefit analysis to determine if that is the correct strategy given the property's condition, as well as real estate market conditions. The property should be appropriately maintained until it is sold.

Assigning Responsibilities

You might want to handle all or some of the items discussed in this chapter yourself, have your team handle them, or ask your agent to manage them for you. An experienced agent should be able to help take over any or all of these pre-marketing tasks.

Rekeying and Securing the Property

Once the property becomes vacant, securing the property is very important to prevent squatters and prior occupants or anyone else who may have the key from returning and occupying the property. The prior occupant(s) may still have a copy of the keys. Rekey all exterior doors to the same keycode as the front door, so only one key is needed for access. Also, make sure all gates have locks on them. The locksmith may install a small keyless padlock if required on the gates. A lockbox containing the new key to the front door should also be installed in an inconspicuous location, such as behind foliage or branches of a bush or tree. It can be installed on a pipe either in the front or side of the property. The lockbox is installed to provide access for vendors.

Depending on the history of the property's security, you may decide you need to secure the property with an alarm system, either with or without cameras, to deter squatters. If squatter activity is still an issue with the alarm system, you may decide you need to board up the property with either clear or steel, board up of windows and doors. Another option is to hire a 24/7 security guard to protect the property.

Initial Property Inspection

During your agent's initial inspection, your agent should conduct a walkthrough of the interior of all structures, including garage(s), outbuilding(s), storage, interior rooms, and other accessible areas such as the attic or basement. A walkthrough of the property's exterior should also be conducted, including its front, back, and sides. Exterior and interior photos of the property should be taken, and the following items should be investigated and noted:

- Interior condition.
- Status of all utilities.

- Health and safety issues.
- Habitability issues.
- Exterior condition.
- Yard maintenance.

Your agent should take photos of all personal property as well as health and safety, and habitability issues. Health and safety issues, such as broken glass, leaking roof, or trip hazards, must be handled with a sense of urgency. Habitability issues include rodents or pests and any plumbing, electricity, and gas-related problems that prevent them from being in good working order.

Ask your agent to collect the mail for you, speak with the neighbors, and obtain their contact information. Your agent can provide a business card to the neighbors as well, to inform your agent in cases of emergency at the property.

Personal Property Disposition

You will decide who will handle the disposition of personal property. Either you or one of your team members will handle it, or you can delegate it to your agent to coordinate a personal organizer's services. The personal property left behind should be documented and photographed. The list of personal property should be reviewed with the heirs or beneficiaries to determine what should be disposed of, and what should be sold, either in an estate sale, or an auction sale. If it is determined that some or all of the items left behind are trash and should be disposed of, your agent can obtain bids from trash out vendors.

Utilities

Utilities should be turned on before the property's initial cleaning since water and electricity will be needed. If utilities cannot be turned on for some reason, for example, due to a safety hazard, this term should be specified in your counters to buyers' offers.

When turning on the water, you or your representative should be present at the property to prevent water damage from any pre-existing leaks or faucets that have previously been left turned on. Utilities should be turned off on the day of closing. A final bill and a final meter reading should be requested.

Initial and Ongoing Maintenance

The goal of initial and ongoing maintenance is to protect and preserve the property and limit your liability while making the property as appealing as possible so it can be sold at the highest possible price for your client. It is important to ensure the property is safe to visit and tour, get the property looking and smelling good both on the interior and exterior, and remove any distractions to make the property appealing. It is a turn-off for buyers to tour a property and see trash, dirt, and experience foul odors. The property you are selling should be presented in its best light, look clean and tidy, have a pleasant smell, and be safe to tour.

Initial and Ongoing Sales Clean

If repairs are not being made, the next step is to complete the property's thorough and deep cleaning. That includes all or some of the items listed below, at your discretion:

- Sweep and mop floors.
- Vacuum and shampoo carpets.
- Remove cobwebs from ceilings, walls, and corners.
- Wipe down cabinets, sinks, and countertops.
- Vacuum inside of cabinets.
- Clean inside and outside all appliances. Remove appliances not in working order, if it is possible without damage to the countertop.
- Wash windows and clean ledges.
- Clean mirrors.
- Clean bathtubs, showers, and commodes.
- Clean vents to ensure they are dust-free.
- Clean ceiling fans.
- Clean fireplace(s).
- Install air fresheners, so the property smells fresh and clean.
- Clean gutters and downspouts.
- Power wash the exterior.

Ongoing cleanings can be established with a trusted vendor. If the property will be renovated, the final cleaning is completed after the renovation.

Initial and Ongoing Yard Maintenance

The goal initially is to handle the initial cleanup that has been delayed, to give the property its best appearance. The initial yard maintenance includes removing debris, cutting the grass, removing weeds, trimming down overgrown bushes and plants to make the property more visible and presentable. Either weekly or bi-weekly maintenance should be scheduled to maintain the property until it is sold. It is crucial to schedule ongoing service to prevent potential overgrowth and code violations.

Initial and Ongoing Pool Maintenance

The goal initially is to ensure the pool is not a health and safety hazard. Identify the local requirements for pool safety and adhere to those requirements. Some cities or counties may require swimming pools to be covered and with pool enclosure such as a fence with locked gates. They may also require spas and hot tubs to be covered. The pool and spa must be cleaned, and ongoing maintenance should be scheduled to prevent them from turning green and hazardous.

Initial and Ongoing Handling of Safety and Habitability Issues

Any health and safety, and habitability issues should be addressed immediately:

- Non-working light fixtures
- Broken glass
- Trip hazards
- Plumbing leaks

- Leaking roof
- Rodents or pests
- Lack of, or non-operating smoke and carbon monoxide detectors
- Water heater lacking the appropriate strapping

The appropriate vendor's services should be secured, whether it is a plumber, a retrofitting company to ensure all state and local laws are adhered to, or a pest control vendor. Any of the above issues should be handled as soon as possible to preserve the property and limit your liability.

Initial Winterization

Winterization can help to deter property damage from leaks and water loss. In areas where temperatures drop below freezing, 32 degrees Fahrenheit, winterization is required on vacant properties to protect the plumbing system and its components. Water expands when it freezes, and this expansion generates enough pressure to burst pipes and fixtures. Pipes in crawl space, attics, and unheated rooms are susceptible to freezing. When those pipes thaw, flooding may occur, causing water damage to the property.

A licensed plumber should properly winterize the property to meet local requirements. The process includes a thorough and complete draining of all plumbing and wet heating systems. An air pressure system may be used to clear the system and the use of non-toxic antifreeze. For wet heat systems/radiant heat, the house boiler system needs to be drained, and radiator vents opened. The radiant piping must be drained and blown dry by compressed air and antifreeze added to the pipes. For wells, the tank and pump must be drained and winterized according to local ordinances and regulations. For sump pumps, the electricity must remain on to help ensure the property is not damaged.

The thermostat setting must be high enough to maintain the desired temperature of 55 degrees Fahrenheit in remote locations of the house in the winter to prevent pipes in interior walls from freezing. De-winterization must be completed before buyer inspections and re-winterization after the inspection. The party who will pay for these costs should be identified and negotiated during the offer negotiations process.

Ongoing Snow Removal

In areas where there is snow, it is important to adhere to local code requirements related to snow and ice removal to avoid potential code violations, and ongoing services should be established with a trusted vendor.

To protect others' safety and minimize liability and risks of injury, the sidewalks and driveways should be treated and snow removal completed. Most of the time, a 30-inch-wide path must be cleared in front of the property, up from the street, to access doors and the garage.

The product "ice melt" should be used as added protection for the property. It attracts moisture and forms brine, a salt-water solution. This solution generates heat, which in turn melts the ice. Ice melt comes in various compositions, including calcium chloride, magnesium chloride, potassium chloride, sodium chloride, and urea. Ice melt lowers the freezing temperature of water. The process of attracting water and forming a brine produces heat that, in turn, melts the snow. Ice melt should be applied before storms and snowfall to simplify ice and snow removal.

Initial Removal of Distractions

Your agent should identify any interior and exterior distractions of the property and suggest their removal. This refers to anything that can be interpreted as a part of the previous occupant's presence on the property, or any item that detracts from the property's marketability and appeal.

Examples of interior distractions include non-neutral drapes and curtains, decorative wall plates, creative cabinets, wallpaper, borders, custom paint, shower curtains, decorative ceiling fans and light fixtures, window clings, wall decals, and stickers.

Examples of exterior distractions include tree hazards, wind chimes, hanging plants, lawn sculptures, and the previous occupant's name on the property.

Ongoing Handling of Emergencies

Your agent should respond quickly when emergencies are identified and provide you with detailed photographs and descriptions when they arise. Damage to the property may occur from vandalism or nature, such as wind damage to roof shingles, lightning damage to a tree, or earthquake damage to a swimming pool. Your agent should report these damages and provide you with photos of the damages. These damages should be reported to your insurance agent so an insurance claim can be filed.

The following situations must be handled on an emergency, immediate basis by your agent:

- Unsecured Doors or Windows, Gates, Fences – secure by closing and locking or boarding up.
- Leaking Roof – place a tarp immediately.
- Flooding – the water should be pumped out immediately and affected areas dried.
- Plumbing Leaks – shut off the water at the main valve in the home or at the meter.
- Wet or Moldy Carpeting – remove the carpet.
- Fallen Tree – remove the tree and secure damaged area(s).
- Unsecured Pool – cover and ensure fence and gate have control access.
- Fire – secure property by boarding up and fencing.

Renovations

A cost/benefit analysis should be conducted to determine if it makes sense to renovate the property. This involves analyzing the neighborhood comparables, the active, pending, and sold within the past 12 months. Review the renovation standards used in comparables of properties that were renovated. Pay attention to the materials and brands of the appliances to determine your renovation project's cost. The upgrades should meet the buyers' expectations of that market. All health and safety issues should be addressed along with section one termite repairs and all liens, code violations, and assessments, if applicable. This will ensure that both conventional and FHA financing can be obtained and accommodate the owner-occupant type of buyer, which is an emotional type of buyer.

Make sure that the property is not being under-improved or over-improved for the neighborhood. It is also important to order a home inspection and termite inspection as part of the cost/benefit analysis to determine the extent of repairs needed and whether the return is great enough, given the costs to repair. If renovating the property, the renovation should make the property turnkey or move-in ready.

Chapter 7: Valuing the Property

Chapter Overview

Pricing your residential or commercial property competitively and accurately is crucial in selling the property for the highest possible price. Your agent must be fluent in preparing CMAs / BPOs and BOVs and not use an automated system to determine a property's value.

Chapter Outline

Introduction

Broker Price Opinion (BPO) aka Competitive Market Analysis (CMA)

Broker Opinion of Value (BOV)

Determining a List Price

Introduction

Pricing the property correctly is key in obtaining the highest possible offer for the property. Pricing the property competitively will generate lots of demand, and a high level of demand will increase the buyers' interest levels and push the price up. Your agent must conduct a thorough analysis of the MLS data for residential properties, or Costar for commercial properties, to arrive at the correct pricing.

Broker Price Opinion (BPO) AKA Comparative Market Analysis (CMA)

You should expect to receive a Broker Price Opinion (BPO), otherwise known as a Comparative Market Analysis (CMA) from your agent. Your agent should not use fully automated software to generate a Comparative Market Analysis (CMA). Pricing analysis requires human intervention. For example, suppose the CMA software searches for comparables within a one-mile radius of the subject property. In that case, it uses values from irrelevant properties that are not comparables, for example, those in lower-priced neighborhoods. For instance, if the subject property is located on the edge of the City of Beverly Hills, searching for comparables within a one-mile radius will pick up properties situated nearby in the bordering City of Los Angeles, City of West Hollywood or both, which will reduce the proposed listing price of the subject property. Proper pricing requires human intelligence to do the thinking and analyzing.

Many agents use automated tools to generate reports with comparables and opinions of value. There are currently no tools on the market to provide the right comparables for each situation and provide a realistic value. An accurate BPO/CMA requires human intelligence to research, analyze, and determine a proposed list price.

The risk with an automated report is that much of the time, it leads you to believe that the value is higher than what it is. The report is then used as the basis for pricing the property, and as a result, the property sits on the market for a while, which usually has a negative impact on the value.

The BPO/CMA prepared by your agent should include 2-3 sold comparables, 2-3 active comparables, along with an analysis of how each of these comparables compares to the subject property. There should be a discussion of which sold and active comparables are most appropriate and why. The BPO/CMA should also include a discussion of the subject property's positive features and the street and neighborhood. Finally, the report should specify any price adjustments and estimated cost of renovations, the proposed list price, and the likely sales price.

Your agent should identify the proper comparables three to six months old, based on location, square footage, bed/bath count, lot size, view, and condition. The comparables' location should be as close as possible to the subject property's location, within a one-mile radius, and farther on rural properties. Appropriate adjustments should be made and accounted for. For example, if the property is located next door to a commercial property, there should be a downward adjustment in the pricing since that makes the property less desirable. Your agent should highlight the positive aspects of the property, for example, if the property is/has:

- Located on a cul-de-sac
- Located in a desirable school district

- Walking distance to a school
- In close proximity to restaurants, stores, banks, etc.
- A large lot size
- A view
- Any renovation completed

A review of the days on market (DOM) and listing price of the active comparables will indicate how well the comparable is priced relative to the market.

Broker Opinion of Value (BOV)

The BOV is used for valuation of commercial real estate. Commercial real estate is categorized into the following categories: multifamily (5+ residential units), retail, land, office, and industrial. Your agent should use Costar data to determine the accurate list price for the property. Costar is the leading authority in commercial data nationwide. Make sure that your agent has access to this data. Most residential agents do not have access to Costar, as the subscription fee is very high.

Some of the MLS systems allow you to list some types of commercial properties, such as multifamily. However, the MLS does not include comprehensive commercial real estate data as it is not widely used and accepted by the commercial real estate community. Using the data available on the MLS to create the BOV will likely lead to an incorrect list price since the analysis would be based on partial data.

It is optimal to utilize an agent specializing in commercial real estate or a boutique brokerage specializing in commercial and residential real estate and has a CoStar subscription. If your agent does not list your commercial property on CoStar, you risk limiting your asset's exposure.

Determining a List Price

Once you have reviewed either the BPO/CMA or BOV, the next step is to determine the list price. A review of the comparables should lead you to a decision. Let's take a hypothetical example:

If three properties similar to the subject property sold for $800k, $815k, and $840k in the past three months within 0.25 miles of the subject, what should the listing price be?

The answer depends on how quickly you want to get into escrow. It is optimal to price the property competitively from the get-go and not have to make reductions. A property with lower days on market is more appealing to buyers.

The lower your list price, the more likely you are to have more eyes look at the property, which is expected to result in more offers. With greater demand comes greater desire to obtain a property, and that's when prices can escalate higher and higher. If your agent is an aggressive negotiator, they will know how to push the offer amounts higher and higher once there is a multiple offer situation.

Comparing based on price per SF (square foot) is another way to arrive at a likely sale price for a property. Find Sold and Active comps, record their sold and list prices per SF and average them. Then, multiply these average prices per SF by the total SF of your subject property to arrive at the likely list and sale prices. Alternatively, you can price the property as low as the lowest sold comparable.

Ultimately, the most important aspect of real estate is pricing. Properties sit on the market because the price is wrong. Properties move when they are priced correctly. Using the proper pricing strategy is critical in the real estate sales process. The correct strategy will generate the highest-priced offer possible for the sale of your real estate asset.

Once a price has been set, your agent should be proactive in monitoring the market. If there is a new listing in the area, the agent should evaluate its pricing and the market's response and determine whether a price reduction is needed given this new data. Suppose there is no activity in the first couple of weeks. In that case, I suggest making a downward price adjustment to generate more interest and excitement, which will likely lead to a multiple offer situation. A multiple offer situation gives your agent the ability to announce to all interested buyers that there is a multiple offer situation and request that they submit their "highest and best" with a specified deadline. This creates pressure for the prospective buyers, and the emotional buyers will offer as much as possible if they have a strong desire for the property. When there is demand, it creates desire, which pushes the price up as high as possible. Your agent should set a deadline for the interested buyers to submit their highest and best.

Chapter 8: Marketing the Property

Chapter Overview

Marketing your property is a critical component of the real estate sales process. Your agent should be diligent in defining a multi-pronged marketing strategy that utilizes as many marketing channels as possible. The goal is to cast the broadest net possible to draw as many eyes on the property and ultimately generate the highest possible sales price. Your agent should be diligent in documenting all buyers who are inquiring about the property, conducting the proper follow-up to bring buyers closer to making an offer, and driving those buyers to come to the courtroom and overbid on a situation requiring court confirmation.

This chapter discusses the various marketing channels and components that deliver a comprehensive marketing solution to limit your liability and ensure your real estate sales success.

Chapter Outline

Introduction

Signage

Professional Photos of Property

Property Description

Professional Video and 3D Virtual Tour

Professional Website

Placing Property on MLS, Loopnet, Costar

Listing Printout

    Public Remarks

    Private Remarks

    Showing Instructions

Showing Properties

Conducting Open Houses

Traditional Marketing

Online Marketing

Handling Price Reductions

Introduction

Marketing is the cornerstone of selling real estate. There are various channels for marketing the real estate being sold, and they are discussed in this chapter. Ultimately, the goal is to get as many eyes looking at the property being sold, and these channels increase the number of eyes. The more eyes that are looking at the property, the lower the risk of underselling. The greater the number of eyes leads to a competitive environment. It initiates offers, which are then driven to provide the maximum possible purchase price with a request for the highest and best offer. Ultimately, this approach delivers the highest possible sales price to the seller.

Multichannel marketing increases the speed of the sale of the property and leads the property to be sold at the absolute maximum price. Knowing that your agent is executing all possible channels to market the property provides you with a sense of assurance that you deliver the highest return rate on the sale for your clients.

Signage

Installing a real estate sign is one of the most effective marketing strategies available for selling real estate. The sign should be installed as soon as the listing agreement is fully executed. As a first step, your agent should conduct the necessary due diligence before ordering a sign: contact the city, and the Homeowner's Association (HOA), if there is one, to determine what the signage requirements are.

Standard residential real estate signs are 2'x3' on an 8 ft post, and commercial signs vary. Some cities have restrictions on the post's height, while other cities will have requirements for the size of the sign and the type of frame used. Other cities do not permit signs to be installed at all. The same kinds of rules would apply with an HOA. Your agent should conduct this necessary due diligence and then order the correct type of signage to be installed. Otherwise, the city or HOA can issue a fine. The sign should be installed once you sign the listing agreement, and you can request that your agent email you a photo confirming that it was installed.

Some agents pre-market their listings to their network of investors and go under contract before executing all marketing strategies and before even installing a sign. This is a red flag. You need your agent to offer the property to the open market for a sufficient amount of time, at a minimum of ten calendar days. The sign should be installed, and the property's exposure should be opened up to all marketing channels to bring offers at market value and ensure the property is not being undersold.

Professional Photos of Property

"A picture is worth a thousand words." What a true statement, especially when it comes to selling real estate. Buyers are browsing the internet for homes to buy, and if they like the photos, they take the next step in requesting to see the property. Your agent should have a professional photographer on their extended team, ensuring that a sufficient number of marketable photos are available before placing the property on the market. Homes with more photos sell faster. According to a study conducted by the National Association of Realtors, homes with one photo spend an average of 70 days on the market, and a home with 20 photos spends an average of 32 days on the market. Those with professional photos also sell for more.

Once the property has been prepared for photography, whether it's just a trash out, sales clean, and yard cleanup, or renovations and landscaping to bring the property current, your agent should arrange for professional photos to be taken. If the property is occupied and the occupant is cooperative with providing access, the property will not be cleaned up, and the professional photos will include the occupant's personal property. If the occupant is not cooperative and will not provide access, then exterior photos only should be taken by the photographer.

Interior photos should include multiple pictures of each room: bedrooms, bathrooms, kitchen, living room, family room, den, utility room, and garage. In addition, photos of the systems should be taken: appliances and heating and air conditioning systems. Interior pictures of any detached structures such as garages or Accessory Dwelling Units (ADUs) should be taken as well.

Exterior photos include the property's frontal view, with and without the real estate sign, and pictures of the side yards, backyards, left-side and right-side views of the house, pool/spa, and any other favorable features of the property. Suppose there is a favorable feature in the neighborhood, such as a peaceful park walking distance away. In that case, the photographer should take photos of the park to give the prospective buyer a true feel for the property and the neighborhood.

Your agent should email you a link to all of the photos the photographer takes to have historical documentation and provide transparency and make sure you know which photos are being used for marketing the property.

Property Description

The property description should be both honest and accurate and also draw a buyer's attention. Your agent should use their creativity to describe the property, focusing on turning flaws into a positive opportunity to improve. If the property needs work and is a fixer, the property should mention that so prospective buyers know what to expect and don't waste their time.

The description should not be in ALL CAPS. The goal is not to intimidate and irritate potential buyers and buyers' agents but to be friendly, inviting, and easy to work with.

You may request a copy of the MLS printout, the agent detail version, from your agent so that you can review the property description, the public, and private remarks.

An accurate description that focuses on the property's positive features will draw buyers interests to look at the video, the tour, photos and get them closer to requesting a showing.

Professional Video and 3D Virtual Tour

In general, research has shown that providing prospective buyers with a professional video and a 3D virtual tour available at their fingertips, in the comfort of their homes, will generate greater interest from buyers and results in more property showings.

A professional video generates much more interest in the property than just having photos available for prospective buyers. The prospective buyer remains more engaged in viewing the property online with a video and for an extended period, leading to greater interest and more buyers interested in visiting the property. Agents offer various types of videos. Some agents assemble photos taken of the property and include background music. Other agents have a professional video produced while walking through the property and marketing the property's positive features. It allows prospective buyers to feel like they are walking through the home.

A 3D virtual tour will increase the property's visibility and provide buyers a realistic view of the property's interior and exterior. The 3D virtual tour allows a buyer or buyer's agent to walk through the property virtually and zoom in and inspect all rooms as well as the exterior of the property.

Professional Website

High-valued properties, luxury properties that are not fixers, typically warrant a professional website. This is an industry-standard. The website should include professional photos, video(s), a 3D virtual tour, a property description, and the listing agent's contact information.

Placing Property on MLS, LoopNet, CoStar

The MLS, Loopnet, and Costar are databases that agents use to market properties they have for sale and allow agents to search for properties that meet their buyer clients' search criteria. MLS systems have a specialized focus on residential real estate, yet they allow your agent to enter and market commercial properties. Loopnet and Costar specialize in commercial real estate, and your agent should submit the property listing to these databases when marketing a commercial property.

The listing should include professional photos, a video of the property, a link to the 3D tour, and a link to the property website (for high-valued properties).

Once a property is placed on the MLS, it then propagates to Zillow, Realtor.com, and 100+ other websites that buyers are likely to search, increasing its online visibility.

It is crucial to place your residential properties on the MLS, and the commercial properties on Loopnet and CoStar and the MLS since it allows for maximum property exposure to agents and the relevant buyer pool.

Many agents set up their buyer clients with automated email notifications for properties that match their search criteria within these databases. When a property comes on the market and fits the buyer's search criteria, the buyer receives an automated email from the database with the property details.

Listing Printout

To verify the listing's accuracy, you can request a copy of the MLS, Costar, and Loopnet printouts to be emailed to you as a PDF file. Request the "Agent Detail" version, so you can check the private remarks and showing instructions. Verify that the property address and property type are correct and that the property description, square footage, and bed/bath count are accurate. The listing should specify if court confirmation is required. There should be multiple attractive and clear exterior and interior photos.

Public Remarks

The public remarks should focus on the property's positive features, including repairs and updates made to the property, location, and neighborhood amenities.

The public remarks should be updated once the court hearing date has been established on a limited authority sale requiring court confirmation. The minimum first overbid price should be specified along with the date and location of the court hearing.

Private Remarks

The private remarks field should include instructions on submitting offers and the appropriate real estate forms to be used. Your agent should specify a deadline to submit offers. This creates a sense of urgency among the buyers' agents and buyers. Suppose there is not sufficient activity on the property after a couple of weeks. In that case, a price reduction can be made to generate additional interest, and a new offer submission deadline is set. Any comments regarding access restrictions to the property due to environmental hazards, for example, should be noted in the private remarks, not the public remarks.

Showing Properties

The showing instructions field should include requirements to qualify buyers before authorizing access to the property. The buyer's agent should submit valid and current proof of funds and a pre-approval letter showing that the buyer is qualified to purchase the property. Your agent should request verification that the buyer has viewed the 3D-tour available on the MLS before scheduling a showing of the property. Once the prospective buyer has confirmed viewing the 3D-tour and is qualified, the seller's disclosure package should be provided to the buyers' agents for buyers' review. This package includes any inspection and pre-sale reports, the goal is to disclose all known material facts upfront. This procedure ensures that only qualified and interested buyers have access to the property. It saves time for everyone involved.

On a vacant property, your agent should carefully evaluate the situation to determine whether an electronic lockbox should be installed for showings or not. If, for example, there is a security system installed because there was previously a break-in, or the area has had squatter activity, your agent should not install an electronic lockbox and show the property by appointment only to safeguard the property. If an electronic lockbox is installed, agents representing buyers use it to access the property and conduct showings. Installing it allows for greater flexibility. Only licensed real estate professionals are authorized to access electronic lockboxes. Buyers are not authorized to access lockboxes, and their agents must accompany them during the property showing.

An occupied property should not have a lockbox installed for security and privacy reasons. The showing instructions on occupied properties must be by appointment only and coordinated with the occupant's availability.

Every opening of the electronic lockbox is recorded and your agent can generate a report to review the showing activity. This allows your agent to keep track of agents with interested buyers and keep them informed of the property's updates. Your agent should follow up with these agents throughout the sales process:

- Limited Authority Situation: once a court hearing date has been established to invite their clients to overbid in court.

- Full Authority Situation: when there is a price reduction to activate more interest.

Conducting Open Houses

Your agent should conduct at least two open houses to allow buyers and other agents the opportunity to view the property. In a transaction with limited authority, the judge will want to ensure that the property was marketed adequately with at least two open houses. Virtual open houses are encouraged, and if the client is still interested in the property after viewing the virtual open house, your agent should schedule a showing. Your agent should implement the safety precautions and guidelines prescribed by the C.A.R. (California Association of Realtors) to limit your liability.

If conducting open houses, each open house should be advertised on the MLS (from there, it is propagated to Zillow and other real estate websites). You may request that your agent provide you with a photo of the Open House sign-in sheets, proving that the open houses were conducted and gauging the buyer's interest level in the property.

Traditional Marketing

Your agent should create a property flyer. You may request to review and approve it. The agent should place several color property flyers at the property, preferably on the kitchen counter. If printing out and leaving property flyers at the property are discouraged, to maintain health and safety requirements, e-flyers are used instead.

Depending on whether you have worked with your agent before or not, and your trust level, you may request that your agent email you any flyers for review and approval before printing and distributing them. When an open house is conducted, your agent should create and print professional open house flyers and share them with you.

Other traditional marketing channels include ads in local newspapers and specialized magazines, which would apply to specialized and luxury properties. Most buyers are browsing online, so marketing in newspapers and magazines primarily benefits the real estate agent and not the property.

Online Marketing

To further increase the property's visibility, your agent should market the property on the agent's website. Your agent should also create an e-flyer and email it to their network of agents and buyers. Your agent should be building a database of agent and buyer contacts to maximize exposure each time a new property is being sold.

Your agent should have visibility in social media, including LinkedIn, Facebook, Instagram, and Twitter, and the property should be marketed within these platforms.

Handling Price Reductions

Your agent should monitor the activity level of each property that is on the market and update you. The goal is to limit the number of days on market (DOM) and generate enough activity to activate a multiple offer situation. If the activity level is insufficient, your agent should provide suggestions for change and provide data supporting it.

If there is no or very little activity during the first two weeks of listing the property on the market, it is very likely that the price is wrong, in other words, overpriced and not priced competitively. Your agent should be proactive in monitoring the activity and proposing a price reduction to generate sufficient showing activity and create a multiple offer situation. Your agent should suggest a new and reduced listing price and provide you with comparables that support the reduction being proposed. If you approve of the price reduction, your agent should complete the Modification of Listing, Buyer Representation, or Other Agreement Between Principal and Broker (C.A.R. Form MT) with the new listing price and send it to you for review and signature. Once it is fully executed, the MLS, Loopnet, and Costar, should be updated with the new price. Your agent should follow up with all agents and buyers who previously inquired about the property to update them on the current price.

Chapter 9: Purchase Agreement Terms

Chapter Overview

Key terms which appear in real estate purchase agreements are reviewed and interpreted in this chapter.

Chapter Outline

Introduction

As-Is Sales

Investigations

Warranties, Guarantees, or Representations

Requests for Repairs

Retrofitting Repairs

Escrow, Title, and Natural Hazard Disclosure (NHD) Vendors

Earnest Money Deposit

Buyer Inspections and Investigations

Court Confirmation Contingency

Extension of Time Addendum and Per Diem Fee

Introduction

Your agent will need to be familiar with the process to define the proper contract terms during the offer negotiations process. The terms help to protect the seller and ensure a smooth escrow process. Your agent should also understand the market and the type of buyer that will pay most for the property and customize the contract terms accordingly to accommodate the right type of buyer. Your agent should review and discuss these terms with you prior to initiating marketing of the property. The terms are identified in the paragraphs below. Each term is presented in bold and then explained.

As-Is Sales

Sale to be As-Is - What does it mean to sell a property in "As-Is" condition? It's a boundary that the seller is setting, stating that the seller is not willing to entertain any requests for repairs or credits during escrow. Many buyers see this term and still proceed with their requests for credits and repairs. To protect yourself, make sure your agent has a call with the buyer and buyer's agent before offer acceptance to explain to them that you are not willing to entertain any requests for repairs or credit. If these requests are made during escrow, the seller will move on to the next buyer.

At the close of escrow, the buyer purchases the property in its existing condition as of the date of offer acceptance. The seller is not obligated to repair defects that exist as of the date of offer acceptance and is not willing to entertain a buyer's request for repairs or credit.

The seller does have to disclose known material defects. Some sellers have a misconception that if they are selling "As-Is," they do not need to discuss the leaking roof or other material facts they are aware of since it is being sold "As-Is." This is not true. The seller is obligated to share any known knowledge, anything that they are aware of, about the property, which might affect a buyer's buying decision. This is legally required, even in fiduciary managed transactions. If the seller fails to disclose a known material fact about the property, and the buyer finds out after the close of escrow that the seller was aware, the seller can be held liable. The buyer can learn about a situation from a neighbor, or, from review of city or police records. Better to be honest and over disclose than fail to disclose and take on that liability.

The seller is also responsible for maintaining the property in the condition it was in on the date of offer acceptance. This includes maintenance of the landscaping and grounds and the pool and spa. As-Is does not mean you take the property as you find it on the date of close of escrow, but instead, the condition it was in on the date of offer acceptance. The buyer can conduct the desired investigations – to inspect the property, determine the condition by reviewing the seller's disclosures and having inspections conducted to discover the property's true condition.

Selling As-Is does not mean that the seller can leave trash and personal property inside the property. If the seller chooses not to do a property cleanout by removing the trash and personal property, then that specific term must be countered from the purchase agreement. Unless this is negotiated out of the contract during the offer negotiations process, the seller must remove all trash and personal property from inside the garage, closets, sheds, and detached structures.

Your agent should arrange to remove all trash and personal property and do a deep cleaning before placing the property on the market. The property will be more visually appealing and will have a more desirable scent. The property will appeal to more buyers. This, in turn, will maximize the return on the sale.

Investigations

Buyer shall conduct all investigations to satisfy self - This term makes it clear that the buyer has the right to inspect the property.

Warranties, Guarantees, or Representations

No warranties, guarantees, or representations regarding the adequacy, condition, performance, suitability of the property or its' systems or components are expressed or implied - This term protects the seller from any future claims from the buyer regarding any property's systems or components.

Requests for Repairs

No request for repair will be considered, and no credits will be given - This term further reinforces the "As-Is" sale, making it clear that the seller will not consider a Request for Repair or Credit.

Retrofitting Repairs

All retrofitting repairs required to be made before the close of escrow as a result of local and state laws shall be paid for by Buyer, using Seller's choice of vendor - The seller's choice of vendor limits the liability to the seller. It allows the seller to control the vendor completing the work since the seller has a relationship with the vendor. The seller can also verify that the vendor is qualified and adequately insured. The seller can ensure the repairs are completed correctly and in compliance with local and state laws. The seller is still the owner of the property during the escrow period. Therefore, the seller bears the responsibility for the vendors performing work on the property, and the seller's choice of vendors should be used.

Escrow, Title, and Natural Hazard Disclosures (NHD) Vendors

Seller's choice of vendor for escrow and title services, as well as Natural Hazard Disclosures Report - The seller's choice of vendor for escrow and title allows the seller to control the escrow process and to resolve title matters since the seller has a relationship with the escrow and title offices. The same applies to the provider of the Natural Hazard Disclosure report. Per California law, it is the seller's responsibility to deliver the natural hazard disclosures. Therefore, the seller should be the one to select a reputable vendor to provide it and ensure that seller is adhering to state laws.

Earnest Money Deposit

Upon acceptance, Buyer shall provide Seller with a deposit equal to 10% of the purchase price in the form of a cashier's check made payable to the name of the estate and delivered to seller's office - With a limited authority sale, it is customary that the earnest money deposit amount is 10% of the purchase price. It should be provided to the executor or administrator of the estate once there is offer acceptance, subject to court confirmation. If the buyer defaults, the earnest money deposit is available immediately to the estate. If another buyer's offer is accepted as part of the court's overbidding process, the earnest money deposit is available immediately to return to the original buyer.

Buyer Inspections and Investigations

Buyer has completed all Buyer inspections and investigations, Buyer approves condition and status of the property, and all Buyer contingencies referred to in the Agreement are hereby removed and waived - This term protects the seller, making it clear that the buyer was given the opportunity to inspect the property and approves its status and that buyer is removing all contingencies.

Extension of Time Addendum and Per Diem Fee

Suppose the buyer fails to close escrow in the agreed-upon time period. In that case, the seller can petition the court to vacate the sale and seek damages or grant the buyer an extension to complete the sale, provided that the buyer pays a per diem fee to the seller outside of escrow.

An Extension of Time Addendum will be issued, specifying the new Close of Escrow date. The per diem fee must be paid in full at the time that Seller issues the Extension of Time Addendum. The per diem charge shall be $100 for the first seven days granted and $200 for any additional days. Should Buyer close escrow before the Close of Escrow date specified in the Extension of Time Addendum, Seller shall refund to Buyer outside of escrow the portion of the penalty assessed for each full calendar day remaining beyond the actual close date. Buyer acknowledges that nothing in this section grants the Buyer a 'right' to an extension and that the decision to grant an extension is solely within Seller's discretion - This is an important term that applies pressure on the buyer to perform and close on time. It motivates the buyer and buyer's agent to promptly deliver any required documents to the lender and escrow promptly, stay engaged in the escrow process, and not cause any delays in the closing and incur penalty fees, which are charged per day "per diem." It also protects the seller, indicating that buyer is not being granted a right to an extension, and it is at the seller's discretion whether it will be approved.

Chapter 10: Offer Management

Chapter Overview

Proper oversight of the offer management process is critical to a successful real estate sale. Your agent's adoption of the appropriate methodology and procedures will ensure an efficient and error-free sale, saving you time and making the process an easy one for you. Given the nature of sales transactions, it is prudent for your agent to provide the buyer's agent community with offer submission instructions to educate them and identify which contract forms to use and what the acceptable contract terms are.

Your agent should provide you with a summary of offers received and make recommendations on how to respond. Inducing a multiple offer situation when there is only one offer submitted is possible using the proper strategy, which results in generating the highest possible sales price for your client.

Setting the proper buyer expectations before offer acceptance encourages a smoother escrow process. Understanding what you, the seller, and your agent, are required to disclose is critical in mitigating your liability.

Establishing a checklist that ensures all contract components are included in the contract package is critical in being efficient and ensuring there is no oversight and missing documents. Ensuring your agent conducts a detailed contract review before submitting it to you for execution is a required step to avoid errors and cause delays.

Chapter Outline

Introduction

Offer Submission Instructions

Reviewing and Processing Offers

Handling Multiple Offer Situations

The Contract Package

Contract Package Review

Introduction

Management of the offers process is a critical component of the real estate sales process. This chapter is specific to offer management of real estate sales.

In a transaction, your agent needs to take a more detailed approach and provide specific instructions to the buyer's agents on submitting offers to ensure offers comply with real estate sales requirements. It is your agent's responsibility to handhold those agents who do not have prior court confirmed real estate sales experience, guide them through the process, and educate them on acceptable offer terms.

Providing buyer's agents with detailed instructions on how to submit offers makes the process a more efficient one. Having a procedure for reviewing and processing offers makes the offer management process more efficient, accurate, and transparent. It ensures proper recording and record-keeping and ensures that every offer that was submitted is communicated to you, the seller.

Offer Submission Instructions

Your agent should prepare "Offer Submission Instructions" based on your desired contract terms and whether the sale has limited authority, requiring court confirmation, or is full authority, which most of the time does not require court confirmation. Discuss this with your agent and define your expected contract terms before placing the property on the market. You may also request to review your agent's "Offer Submission Instructions" to ensure they comply with your requirements and expectations. This will ensure that the offers submitted comply with your expectations.

The instructions may include:

1. Email the listing agent's office to request a "pre-offer" package, including the seller's disclosures.
2. Status of contingencies, whether they all must be removed or not.
3. Earnest money deposit amount required, to whom it should be payable, and when it should be delivered.
4. Days to close escrow.
5. Which party, seller, or buyer, is to pay for repairs required to be handled before the close of escrow, such as retrofitting repairs.
6. Which party, seller or buyer, is to pay for concessions such as natural hazard disclosures (NHD), termite repairs, or any other lender required repairs.
7. Which party, seller or buyer, will select the vendors to be used for services, such as escrow and title.

Reviewing and Processing Offers

Once your agent begins to receive offers, they should be stored, recorded, and communicated to you. Your agent should ensure that all offers received are vetted appropriately. Your agent should ensure that there is current proof of funds and a pre-approval letter for each buyer and that the buyer has also visited both the interior and exterior of the property, where there is access to the property's interior. If a loan is being obtained, your agent should reach out to the loan officer who issued the pre-approval letter and verify the buyer's qualifications.

Once the offer submission deadline has passed, your agent should report back to you with a summary of all offers received. It should include your agent's recommendation on how to proceed. Communicate this to your agent to allow for a more efficient offer review process.

An offer submitted by a buyer that is a business, trust, LLC, or corporation must include signing authority showing that the signer is authorized to sign on behalf of the entity. If the buyer is a licensed real estate broker or agent, this must be disclosed in the offer. Sometimes a buyer is not aware of this disclosure requirement or forgets to disclose it.

Your agent should confirm whether the buyer is a licensed real estate broker or an agent upon receipt of an offer. The estate is not liable to pay any commission or fee or any other compensation or expenses related to the sale of the property to a broker or agent under the following circumstances:

- If the agent or broker is the purchaser of the property, directly or indirectly.
- If the agent or broker has any interest (e.g., financial interest) in the buyer.

Handling Multiple Offer Situations

If there are multiple offers, your agent should request the highest and best offer using the Seller Multiple Counter Offer form (C.A.R. form SMCO) from all buyers and set a new deadline to respond by. The buyers should submit updated proof of funds and a pre-approval letter if the purchase price is increased. Your agent should record all buyer responses and email you a revised summary with a recommendation on how to proceed. Depending on the responses received and how experienced the buyer is whose offer is highest, there are various ways to respond:

- Accept the highest offer.
- Counter out all or some contingencies: for limited authority sales, all contingencies must be removed, and in full authority sales, which do not require court confirmation, this is not required. Removing the appraisal contingency would require the buyer to increase their down payment if the property does not appraise at the purchase price value. You can also request that the buyer conduct all inspections over a couple of days and remove the inspection contingency at that time.
- Issue a counter at a higher price.

Before accepting an offer, your agent should have a conference call with the buyer's agent and the buyer and set the proper expectations. Suppose there is a multiple offer situation with offers very close to each other in terms of price. In that case, your agent should explain to them that there are many other offers, all very close in terms of price and that if they come back during escrow and request a price reduction, credit, or repairs, the seller will move on to the next buyer.

If there is only one offer, most of the time, it is lower than the asking price. One strategy to consider is to counter the buyer at the asking price. If the buyer does not come up in price, you can request that your agent lower the asking price to what the buyer is offering, expose it to the market, and see if there are any other takers. Set a new deadline for offer submission, say a week out, and welcome the buyer who offered the low price to resubmit the offer if still interested.

Using this strategy, your agent may generate a multiple offer situation and have the opportunity to push the prices up higher.

The Contract Package

Once the final negotiations have been completed, your agent should compile the contract package. The contract package should be compiled in the following order and assembled into a single PDF file:

1. Purchase Agreement
2. Counters and Addendum, in order, most recent on top
3. Proof of Funds (dated in the past 30 days, must include buyer's name, all pages must be included; account statements or signed bank letter are acceptable.)
4. Pre-Approval Letter, if applicable (dated in the past 30 days, must specify if owner occupant)
5. Organizing documents, if the buyer is an entity, such as a corporation or LLC, etc., as a means to show proof of signing authority.
6. Trust documents (if the buyer is a trust).
7. Gift letter (if gift funds are being granted in order to qualify for the purchase)

Contract Package Review

Your agent should take the time to review all of the above documents diligently, look for missing signatures and initials, look for any missing pages, and ensure the contracts have been completed correctly. Your agent should communicate with the buyer's agent to request any missing documents or signatures.

It is vital that your agent is patient and is willing to take the time to go back and forth with the buyer's agent until the contract package is perfect. Otherwise, this will cause delays and may require you to sign the contract again once an error is discovered after the fact. Also, there will be delays with escrow, or the transaction will fall out of escrow if something critical was missed.

Your agent should call the lender who issued the pre-approval letter and confirm the buyer(s) qualifications and confirm that a pre-approval was issued and not just a pre-qualification. A pre-qualification is merely a verbal qualification. The buyer verbally provides financial attributes to the lender to determine a hypothetical purchase price for a particular loan program.

Once the contract package is complete, it should be sent to you for your signature via electronic signing. In the case of full authority, where court confirmation is not required, your agent should issue a Notice to Buyer to Perform (C.A.R. Form NBP) upon offer acceptance to enforce delivery of earnest money deposit by the buyer to escrow on time.

The Notice to Buyer to Perform gives the seller the right to cancel if the buyer does not perform within two days after delivering this form (but no less than the time specified in the agreement). It allows the seller to reassert the need to comply with the contract terms and can be utilized throughout the escrow process to remove contingencies and any contractual action, such as returning the statutory disclosures.

Chapter 11: Closing and Settlement

Chapter Overview

The escrow process in a transaction requires a pre-escrow phase where a lot of due diligence is handled by your agent to avoid closing delays and escrow failure. There is a total of five phases in the escrow process. Each phase includes procedures used to protect the seller of real estate property.

Chapter Outline

Introduction

The Escrow Process

    Pre-Escrow Period Activities (Phase 1)

        Determine Property's Jurisdiction

        Business License Due Diligence

        City Pre-Sale Requirements

        Code Enforcement Due Diligence

        Housing Department Due Diligence

        HOA Due Diligence

        Preliminary Title Report Due Diligence

        Compile Seller's Disclosure Package

        Confirm Utilities On/Turn On Utilities

Order Products and Services

Initial Escrow Period Activities (Phase 2)

    Set Status to "Pending"

    Send "Request to Open Escrow" Email

Intermediate Escrow Period Activities (Phase 3)

    Confirm that Escrow Received Buyer's Deposit

    Ensure Contingencies are Removed

    Repairs Required to be Made During Escrow

    Order Home Warranty Plan

End of Escrow Period Activities (Phase 4)

    Contact Lender to Determine Closing Readiness

    Determine Escrow Office Readiness

    Contact Buyer's Agent to Determine Closing Readiness

    Final Verification of Property Condition

Pending to Sold Activities (Phase 5)

    Reminder to Turn Off Utilities

    Request Lawn/Pool Services to be Terminated

    Remove Sign

    Set Status to Sold

Introduction

The escrow process is a detailed one that should be handled in phases to ensure the execution is organized and effective. Your agent must adhere to the proper procedures to ensure your client's best interests are met and protected. Within each of the five phases, specific activities should be handled promptly. The process launches with a pre-escrow phase that requires your agent to conduct various due diligence activities and sets the foundation for an effective and successful escrow process.

The Escrow Process

Whether real estate is being sold as limited authority case, where court confirmation is required, or full authority case, which most of the time does not require court confirmation, the escrow process is generally the same.

In California, the escrow agent is a neutral third party who holds buyer funds in order to meet the terms and conditions of the written purchase contract between buyer and seller.

The following five phases make up the escrow process, allowing to efficiently and effectively transfer real property between seller and buyer in a transaction. Your agent is a part of your team, and there should be open communication, along with regular weekly updates throughout the escrow process, until the day escrow closes.

Pre-Escrow Period Activities (Phase 1):

Your agent should initiate the "pre-escrow" process once you assign the property as a listing. The escrow officer should be notified. A request should be made for the escrow team to order the Natural Hazard Disclosures (NHD) and any city-required inspections and reports required to be delivered to the buyer prior to close of escrow. If there is a Home Owner's Association (HOA), their contact information should be provided as well. This allows for a quicker and smoother escrow process and enables your agent to deliver all disclosures and documents to prospective buyers before offer negotiations. This is especially important in sales requiring court confirmation, as those offers must have no contingencies prior to the court hearing scheduling.

Determining Property's Jurisdiction

As a first step, your agent should research to determine if the property is located within city limits or in an unincorporated area of the county. A mailing address that specifies a city's name does not necessarily mean the property is located within city limits.

Conducting an internet search of the county's or city's "Geographic Information Systems" will lead to a mapping system where the property address is entered into a search bar, and the results specify the city in which the property is located. Either the city name will be specified, or the property information will specify "city limits." To confirm, when calling one of the city departments referenced below, the city representative can confirm whether the property is indeed located within city limits or not.

This is an important first step. Each city and county have specific requirements related to:

- Business license requirements for real estate licensees when selling property.
- Pre-sale inspection/report requirements.
- Outstanding code enforcement matters.
- Specific housing department requirements related to rent increases and relocation assistance/cash for keys programs.

Business License Due Diligence

Some cities consider the sale of real estate a business activity and require that the real estate licensee obtain a business license. The license is usually valid for one year and requires an application to be completed and submitted, along with a fee. Your agent should call the city's Business License department or unit and inquire if the license is required.

City Pre-Sale Requirements

If the property is indeed located within city limits, your agent should call the city and inquire if there are any pre-sale requirements. The pre-sale requirements vary from city to city, and some cities do not have any pre-sale requirements. Examples of the types of pre-sale requirements cities may have: Report of Building Records in Ventura, Sale of Property Affidavit in Beverly Hills, Smoke Detector Inspection in Palm Springs, Real Property Records Report in Palos Verdes Estates, and in Malibu the Wastewater Treatment System Point of Sale Inspection and the Wastewater Treatment System Transfer of Permit.

This due diligence is critical. Not handling it during the pre-escrow phase will most likely delay the closing. This report is also required to be included as part of the seller's disclosures and provided to prospective buyers. It is especially critical for sales with non-contingent offers so that buyers can review a complete seller's disclosure package before offer negotiations.

Code Enforcement Due Diligence

Your agent should first determine the property's location, whether it is within a city's limits or located in an unincorporated area of a county. The respective jurisdiction's code enforcement department should be contacted to determine if any code violations exist on the property or any outstanding fees. The code enforcement department is responsible for enforcing all the city's and county's laws and ordinances governed by the municipal code.

If code violations exist, your agent should speak with the assigned inspector to request detailed information and requirements to resolve the violation. The inspector should be informed that the property is being sold. Your agent should request confirmation from the inspector that the violation can be transferred to a buyer. The inspector should advise what, if anything, is required to transfer the responsibility of the violation to the buyer.

This information is vital to disclose to prospective buyers so it is clear what they are responsible for and so there are no surprises during escrow, which can cause delays and fallout of escrow.

Housing Department Due Diligence

Your agent should first determine the property's location, whether it is within a city's limits or located in an unincorporated area of a county. The respective jurisdiction's housing department should be contacted to determine if there is rent control and, what the requirements are for offering relocation assistance, or cash for keys to occupants, depending on whether the occupants are at-fault or not. At-fault refers to the occupant's violation of a lease term. The requirements may include specific relocation amounts or your ability to negotiate any amount you would like. There may be a disclosure requirement where certain disclosures must be reviewed and signed by the occupants and returned to the city or county for their records. Your agent should determine whether any documents must be provided to the housing department once cash for keys has been executed and the occupant has vacated the property.

HOA Due Diligence

Depending on the property's location, it may be managed by a Homeowner's Association (HOA). Your agent should conduct the necessary due diligence to determine if there is an HOA. The HOA may be named as part of the legal description. Your agent should research the area where the property is located, determine if there are "sub-districts" and if an HOA manages them. If the property is a condominium, it will most definitely be managed by an HOA. Speaking with the neighbors will help determine if there is an HOA and the HOA name. The HOA usually has a website with contact information that includes an email address.

Your agent should reach out to the HOA and request the following details:

- Monthly dues.
- Services and amenities provided.

- Identify any outstanding issues.
- Identify any outstanding payments.
- Identify if there are regulations on real estate signage related to size and placement: some HOAs require a shorter post or a smaller sign or do not allow a real estate sign to be installed.
- Identify the contact information for the person handling HOA documents and works with escrow.

Preliminary Title Report Due Diligence

Your agent should assist you with getting a clean and clear title, and with the proper vesting, during this phase of the escrow process. Once you assign a property that needs to be sold to your agent, your agent should reach out to the title representative and request to open an order of the preliminary title report. Meet with your agent to discuss the possible chain of title issues and documentation you have to clarify the chain of title. For example, suppose there was a court order indicating that the property should be sold. This documentation should be provided to your agent. Your agent should take the time to review these documents in detail and understand the structure of the court order and the difference between "recitals" and the "terms and settlement" of a court's settlement agreement in preparation for the review of the preliminary title report with the title representative.

Your agent should schedule a time to review the report with the title representative. The chain of title should be reviewed, and any title defects, such as liens, encumbrances, and any other issues that require resolution. A title underwriter will review the preliminary title report and provide a list of conditions to be cleared. Conditions may include recording of a court order or providing supporting documents such as a copy of a death certificate. This due diligence will ensure there are no future claims for the insurer.

If a title company rejects your request for insurance, do not despair. There are title companies that specialize in handling complex situations and are experienced in reviewing and understanding court orders and working through title issues. Your agent should have a network of title insurance providers and should be able to assist you with identifying a provider that will insure it.

Compile Seller's Disclosure Package

Your agent should compile the seller's disclosure package for you to complete and sign during this pre-escrow phase. The package discloses everything related to the property. It is crucial to handle this upfront for a sale requiring court confirmation since the accepted offer must have no contingencies before scheduling the hearing.

Therefore, the usual review of disclosures during the inspection period of a standard transaction with contingencies does not occur. There will not be an inspection contingency, and all inspections, which includes a review of disclosures, must be handled before offer acceptance, and before the scheduling of the court hearing.

Even if the sale is a limited authority that does not require court confirmation, it is prudent to have the disclosures available for prospective buyers to review before offer negotiations. These disclosures most likely will affect the buyers' purchase price being offered and purchasing decision. Any disclosure made to the buyer after offer acceptance provides a buyer with cancellation rights, which means the buyer has the right to cancel and the deposit becomes refundable, even when the offer is non-contingent.

Confirm Utilities On/Turn On Utilities

Confirming that utilities are on at the property should be handled during this pre-escrow phase. Having utilities on not only allows you to clean the property but also to have prospective buyers conduct their inspections. In sales requiring court confirmation, it is imperative to have this handled at this stage. It allows prospective buyers to complete their inspections before submitting their offer with no contingencies.

If it is not possible to have utilities turned on, if, for example, it is unsafe due to plumbing leaks or exposed electrical wires, this should be communicated to prospective buyers. This term should be negotiated out of the purchase agreement when negotiating with a prospective buyer. The default California purchase agreement specifies that the seller will have utilities on for the buyer to inspect.

Order Products and Services

Products such as the Natural Hazard Disclosure (NHD) should be ordered by escrow during the pre-escrow phase of the process to be included with the seller's disclosure package. Suppose there is limited access to the property because it is occupied. It may be beneficial for you to pay for the inspections, such as termite and general home inspection, and have your agent order them at this stage. This will allow them to be included in the disclosure package, and buyers can review them before writing an offer. If there are no funds available to pay for inspections, your agent should have a inspection vendors within their network who are willing to get paid through escrow. Providing the inspection reports to buyers before submitting their offers is especially useful if the property is part of a sale that requires court confirmation since those offers must be non-contingent before scheduling the court hearing.

Initial Escrow Period Activities (Phase 2):

In a sale requiring court confirmation, this phase begins once the court has confirmed the sale. Either the original buyer's offer was confirmed in court, or, another buyer who attended the hearing successfully won the overbid process in court.

In a sale that does not require court confirmation, this phase begins once an offer has been accepted and a fully executed contract has been procured.

This is the beginning of the escrow process. Once the escrow process has begun, several steps must be taken to ensure that the property is ready to be sold. By completing these tasks, your agent helps to ensure a smooth transaction.

Set Status to "Pending"

The Multiple Listing Service (MLS) is the marketing database specializing in residential real estate. Costar and Loopnet are databases specializing in commercial real estate. Depending on your agent's specialty, your agent may be a subscriber to one or all of these databases. As a subscriber, the rules of the MLS, Costar, and Loopnet must be adhered to. The

MLS status must be set to "Pending" within 24 hours of being under contract.

Send "Request to Open Escrow" Email

A leadership role must be taken to facilitate the escrow process, and your agent should be the one to do it. Your agent should take a leadership role in facilitating the escrow process. On the day that the fully executed contract is received, your agent should prepare an email to send to the buyer's agent and the escrow officer. The email includes all parties' contact information and a summary of contract terms. The fully executed contract should be included as an attachment. You can ask your agent to forward a copy of the email to you for your records.

Intermediate Escrow Period Activities (Phase 3)

By executing the tasks related to this escrow phase, your agent ensures that the buyer is serious about proceeding with the purchase. Your agent must take an assertive, leadership role to ensure the buyer does not waste time and delay the closing.

Confirm that Escrow Received Buyer's Deposit

Your agent should issue a Notice to Buyer to Perform (C.A.R. Form NBP) upon offer acceptance, enforcing the buyer's contractual obligation to deliver the deposit per terms of the contract.

If the property being sold requires court confirmation, the buyer's deposit, in the form of a cashier's check, must be delivered either to the attorney or to you, the fiduciary, within one business day of offer acceptance, which is subject to court confirmation.

Suppose the property being sold does not require court confirmation. In that case, the buyer's deposit is usually delivered to escrow via a wire within one business day of offer acceptance. Also, if a Notice of Proposed Action (NOPA) is required, it is prepared and served, which allows the heirs/beneficiaries to object to the sale, in which case the sale would require a court hearing, and the court would be required to confirm the sale.

Your agent should follow up to ensure the earnest money deposit was received by the attorney, escrow, or, you, the fiduciary. This is a critical step, as it identifies whether the buyer is serious since the buyer runs the risk of forfeiting the deposit. In a sale requiring court confirmation, by the time the buyer submits the deposit, the offer is non-contingent, and the buyer has no contractual terms allowing to cancel the transaction and retaining the deposit. The buyer whose offer was accepted subject to court confirmation will have the deposit returned only if another buyer, an overbidder, attends the court hearing and has the sale confirmed by the court.

With a sale not requiring court confirmation, the buyer gives up the right to the deposit once the buyer removes all contingencies if the buyer chooses to cancel the transaction. Unless the property condition has changed without remediation from the seller, or, a new disclosure is being made since the buyer's offer was accepted, the buyer does not have cancellation rights. The seller will have the right to keep the buyer's deposit.

For example, suppose there is vandalism at the property after contingencies have been removed, and the condition of the property has changed from the time the offer was accepted. In that case, the seller may remediate the situation by making the proper repairs. If the seller does not remediate, the buyer has cancellation rights that allow for the earnest money deposit to be returned to the buyer.

Ensure Contingencies are Removed

If the property being sold requires court confirmation, the contingencies will already be removed, and this would not apply in this phase.

If the property being sold does not require court confirmation, most of the time, contingencies have not been removed as of yet, and they should be removed during this phase of the escrow process.

The Purchase Agreement specifies the time period for each of the contingencies. There are four contingencies: loan, inspection, appraisal, and title. Other contingencies may be defined in the contract, both by buyer and seller, to which the purchase is subject. The purchase contract is contingent upon the fulfillment of these conditions. According to the Purchase Agreement terms, if any of the contingencies are not fulfilled, the buyer can cancel the contract and escrow and have the earnest money deposit returned to the buyer. Removing contingencies must be done in writing since the Statute of Frauds requires real estate contracts to be in writing to be enforceable. The Contingency Removal Form (C.A.R. Form CR) is used to remove contingencies in writing. By selecting option A.3., the buyer selects to remove any and all buyer contingencies.

Your agent should issue a Notice to Buyer to Perform (C.A.R. Form NBP) to the buyer two days before a contingency removal is due to enforce the buyer's contractual obligation to remove contingencies on time.

Suppose the buyer does not perform and remove contingencies two days after the NBP has been issued. In that case, the seller can proceed with issuing a Cancellation of Contract, Release of Deposit, and Cancellation of Escrow (C.A.R. form CC). Both the contract and escrow can be canceled using this form.

Repairs Required to be Made During Escrow

Your agent should set the proper buyer expectations before offer acceptance, so there are no requests for repairs made during escrow, as discussed in the Offer Management chapter of this book.

The types of repairs that are typical during the escrow process are those that are contractually agreed to between buyer and seller. These include termite repairs, lender-required repairs, and retrofitting repairs as mandated by local and state laws. Some of the local city laws require a pre-sale report, and some require inspections.

If the property being sold requires court confirmation, the typical terms would be for buyer to pay for retrofitting repairs and no other repairs to be made. This is the industry standard. Note that there is no code preventing the seller from making repairs. Given the high deposit amount of 10% of the purchase price customary for sales requiring court confirmation, the typical buyer is an investor, and not an owner occupant who needs the seller to make lender-required repairs to qualify for financing.

If the property being sold does not require court confirmation, the seller may agree to make repairs. The seller should consider that the best offer is the one that provides the highest net purchase price. In some instances, it may be an owner-occupant FHA offer where the buyer is requesting for the seller to make lender required repairs, which may be handled at a low price. A sale without court confirmation gives the seller flexibility in setting the required earnest money deposit amount, which opens up the opportunity to owner-occupant buyers.

Order Home Warranty Plan

The home warranty plan is ordered during this phase of the escrow process. Usually, in a sale requiring court confirmation, the buyer would not be requesting a home warranty plan, and if it was requested, it is typical that the seller would counter it out.

If the sale does not require court confirmation, the terms of the contract may indicate that buyer is requesting a home warranty plan to be paid either by the buyer or seller. Your agent should request the buyer's agent to purchase this plan, using the buyer's choice of vendor, and ensure the cost does not exceed what was specified in the purchase contract. Your agent should provide you with options on addressing the home warranty plan during the offer negotiations process. One option is to indicate, "should Buyer choose to purchase a home warranty plan, Buyer is to pay and select the desired coverage options and plan." The home warranty plan usually covers the repair or replacement of the home's appliances and other major systems such as the HVAC and pool/spa.

End of Escrow Period Activities (Phase 4):

One week before the closing date, your agent should reach out to all parties, the buyer's agent, the lender, and the escrow officer, as a reminder that escrow is scheduled to close in one week. If the buyer is obtaining financing, it is typical that buyer would be getting ready to sign loan documents at this stage, so a reminder and check in on status would let you know whether there will be a delay in closing.

Escrow should also be reminded that the closing date is one week away so they can prioritize their work accordingly. Your agent should request an Extension of Time Addendum (C.A.R. Form ETA) from the buyer's agent if it is not possible to close in one week. The terms of the original contract related to per diem fees should be considered and applied accordingly.

Contact Lender to Determine Closing Readiness

Your agent should reach out to the lender one week before the closing date to request a status update and inquire when buyer is signing loan documents, and determine if there's an expected delay in the closing date. If so, the buyer's agent should be updated and an ETA form provided with the new closing date specified.

Your agent should not accept just any date as the new closing date. Your agent should request a timeline and explanation of what will occur each day, ensure the new closing date is a realistic one, and that the lender, buyer, and buyer's agent are all making an effort to close as soon as possible.

Depending on the contract's original agreed terms, the buyer may be charged a per diem fee for each day that the closing is extended.

To motivate the buyer to perform in a timely manner during escrow, your agent should include a term that charges a per diem fee to the buyer for any delays caused by the buyer in the purchase contract.

Determine Escrow Office Readiness

Your escrow officer is usually managing multiple escrows. It is a good idea to have your agent alert escrow one week before closing to provide an update on when buyers would like to sign loan documents and the proposed funding and recording dates. This will allow your escrow officer to prioritize and ensure the closing deadline can be met.

At this stage, your agent should also:

- Ask escrow if anything is missing, either from the buyer or seller.
- Request to review a copy of the estimated settlement statement. Ensure that vendors who are getting paid through closing have been accounted for. Ensure all entries are accurate.
- Submit any missing invoices from the settlement statement to the escrow officer as soon as possible.

If the transaction is with full authority, and court confirmation does not need to be obtained, ensure that the closing date is not less than 15 days since the NOPA (Notice of Proposed Action) was served to the beneficiaries/heirs.

Contact Buyer's Agent to Determine Closing Readiness

Your agent should reach out to the buyer's agent to confirm that buyer is ready to close in one week and report back findings based on prior follow-ups:

- Any items reported as missing from escrow.
- Update from lender and escrow, such as when the loan documents will be ready for buyer to sign and the proposed funding and recording dates.

Suppose the buyer is not able to meet these milestones. In that case, further communication will be needed amongst all parties, and an Extension of Time Addendum will need to be drawn and executed by buyers and seller.

Final Verification of Property Condition

Your agent should ask the buyer's agent when the final walkthrough will be completed and to provide an executed Verification of Property Condition (C.A.R. Form VP) form once the walkthrough has been completed.

Before the close of escrow, the buyer should complete the final walkthrough to ensure the property's condition has not changed since the buyer's offer was accepted. Once the buyer completes the walkthrough, the buyer documents any previously agreed repairs that were not completed or any change in the property condition since the buyer's offer was accepted. If there is nothing to report, the buyer signs and dates the form, and this serves as confirmation that the buyer has no issues regarding the condition of the property.

If the buyer's agent indicates that the buyer does not wish to conduct a final walkthrough, your agent should still request that the VP form is signed, and the checkbox next to "Buyer waives the right to conduct a final inspection" is checked.

Pending to Sold Activities (Phase 5)

Once your agent notifies you of escrow's confirmation of receipt of recording, which means the property has officially sold, a few final steps need to be taken.

Reminder to Turn Off Utilities

A phone call to the utility companies should be made to turn off utilities as of the date of close of escrow and request a final bill to be mailed to you.

Request Lawn/Pool Services to be Terminated

Either you or your agent should notify the vendor(s) servicing the property: yard maintenance, pool service, and other vendors providing ongoing services. They should be advised that the property has been sold, and their services will no longer be needed. Request a final bill from the vendor(s).

Remove Sign

Your agent should remove the real estate sign from the property.

Set Status to Sold

Your agent should set the status in the MLS, Costar, or Loopnet to "sold" and specify the sold price.

If you have any ideas for improvement of this book or need more information, please email me at orit@GeffenRealEstate.com or text me at 323-606-1919.

If you enjoyed this book, please consider posting a review. Even if it's only a few sentences, it would be a huge help. Thank you.

www.ingramcontent.com/pod-product-compliance
Lightning Source LLC
Chambersburg PA
CBHW070626300426
44113CB00010B/1682